OUT OF THE DREAM PARK

into the revolution of badaserry

sonali sharma

Invincible Publishers

First published in India in 2017 by Invincible Publishers

ISBN: 978-93-86148-82-7

Invincible Publishers
G-120, Sushant Lok III, Sector 57, Gurgaon-122001

Opposite Kasturba Ashram, Radaur Distt Yamuna Nagar, Haryana- 135133

Digitally Printed at Replika Press Pvt. Ltd.

To all the beautiful souls out there who are constantly suffering from contemplations of society. The souls which are holding themselves from being their true self because they are scared of being judged!!And to the power that owns me!

About The Author

* * *

Sonali Sharma is a young beautiful girl. She is a strong woman, who looks at a challenge dead in the eye and gives it a wink. She loves having fun and is adventurous too.

Her unusual precocity finds wrong in nothing. She loves talking to strangers and is not a 'FRIENDS' person.

She enjoys spending time with her family and holds immense gratification for her younger brother. She belongs to a Punjabi family and is quite obsessed about it. She is a loud and lunatic spirit.

Currently, she is studying B Sc (H) in Forensic Science in New Delhi.

Please share your views on this email id :- therevolutionofbadassery@gmail.com

Follow her on Instagram :- @therevolutionofbadassery

Contents

Prologue

❄ ❄ ❄

A little girl, who thought, if she'd break the screen of her television, she'd get to see the manikins of her favourite cartoons!

She thought children were not born before marriage because God had a record of when people got married and he used to gift them with babies only when they got married.

A little girl, who' d always end up hurting her knees whenever she played some game, who' d close her eyes imagining that the world has gone barren and lifeless. She would imagine when she would be dead and she would open her eyes in faint heartedness.

A little girl who would have a pipe dream of Virat Kohli and would wake up in the middle of her dream because she could not get a picture clicked with him for she did not have a camera!

A girl whose first sip of coffee meant getting her tongue burned. A girl, who'd make love to her pillow at night and would actually worry about getting pregnant with the pillow babies.

She would stay out of the group of the gossip-girls because she was never really able to wrap her head around their talks. She would go whole nine yards to get the things she ever wanted.

As she grew up, she found herself caught up in the drama of society. A society, which had a forethought way of having a good life, and a pre-conceived notion about how one should be living.

A society that was always judging her for her dark complexion, her tattooed body, and then judging her for the way she decided to live her life.

People rarely admired her for she was very outspoken.

But, she decided that she won't let any one drag her down. She decided that she won't let herself be dragged to a level of opinion that was as low as theirs. She decided to show them how she was more than the way she looked.

She decided to tell them that the person is from within and not from the skin that lies as the rind on the soul.

She decided to tell them of the power that they all carried within themselves and the power that was guarding them on the outsides.

She decided to tell them that they all could decide the modus-operandi of their life. They all could be the sailors of their ship and all they needed was faith and not hope, for hope is a beggar, "Hope walks through the fire and the faith leaps over it!"; they needed faith in themselves and faith in their powers.

This little girl was grown up now and so were her

thought bubbles. She still continued to have some freakish thoughts and believed in them.

The thoughts, which were limited to games, celebrities, society, now talked of universe, powers, and they even talked of the things which were not visible to our outer eyes. She now had a broader vision to life; she was evolving and is still evolving.

And in the world full of illusions, I find nothing wrong in having an illusion of my own. The life we are living has countless meanings and each one of us has been given all the fair chances to give an individual meaning to this life. The way we sensitize our minds about this life is how it is going to be for us. And no other person can make me apply a black and white filter to my life.

And before I give this game away, let's first have a shout out for you, for being real enough to have a hold of this book. Shout out because you have shown an audacious desire of knowing more about the life we are living unlike the people in our circumambience.

And let's raise a toast for the same beliefs that we will share throughout this book in advance.

Wait here.

I see some spark out there, is that you?

I see a little hurricane and that blend of rainbow in it.

I see that diminutive light, trying to come out of the crevices.

I see some water; half boiling and half frozen. I see a divvy of some huge power!

I see something TINY holding everything big!

You must be my TINY BOI ! Ain't you?

See, I got you!

So, get hearing every time I call your name Tiny.

So, would you walk along with me now?

TINY ! I'm glad that I'll able to share a part of my mind with you in the most felicitous way. I would have got no chance to get you into my thought bubbles if there would have been no writing.

And here I take the lead and I just want you to follow all the way through. Because it is going to be the most arousing journey for you, I know. I've had it once. And this time, I want both of us to get there together.

C'mon follow my lead.....

Listening to the motivational speeches became my time buster. It became my confederate as I travelled my way to college.

It was just another day when I was listening to my favourite and a commendable speaker Mr. Tony Robbins!

His speech went on and I was getting high on it, until I was hit hard.

His voice has always imbued a sense of encouragement in me. It always exalted me, but that day was different.

That day, it stabbed me instead. The speech went on and there came a line that shot me right into my heart like a shotgun.

"If you gotta write a book, write it now."

– Toni Robbins.

I was numb for a moment.

The rest of the speech was now silent. The same line echoed in my head. I had put the video on pause. I could no longer think of anything else, but that one sentence was probably waiting out there for me to hear it.

Before I started listening to the speech that day, I had no goal.

And as this line came over, it it reminded of that it was one of the things that I had envisaged for my future endeavours. It had me in thoughts that why am I not doing it right now?

Within the next few minutes, I jotted down a few headlines that were going to be in my book, and not even a single day after that went by without writing.

A random student, who didn't even know which path was to be taken, because she wasn't aware of her goal, was now turning into a writer.

There are some moments that hold messages for us.

There are certain voices that will exhilarate us and there are certain words that will tell us of what we actually are and they will reveal our reality to us.

Throughout this book, my only aspiration would be to provide you with the thought that you have been disarticulated from, but is actually yours.

A whim that is going to be a key for your success.

May you find that initial push for your dreams.

And here, I would take a moment to render my thanksgiving to Mr. Toni Robbins, who unknowingly became the producer of another book.

[1]

Into her albatraoz life.

* * *

I was the second girl to my parents, they say. And like any other Indian family, people were looking forward for a boy child this time in my family as well.

When it comes to the gender of a newly born baby in a family, most of the Indians want it to be a boy.

And my birth broke all their hopes. Their hopes of procuring a baby boy this time! My mamma was okay with the fact that it was a girl again and so was my dad. But you know, they "Could have been better if..." statement doesn't go away from our lives.

People feigned as if it was a moment of remorse. They were giving their consolations to my family that it'd be a boy next time. It was like they were crying before my parents were hurt. They were bringing up a pain which was not really there.

My parents have never really talked anything about this whole happening, but then my aunt used to say this to me that, "I wanted to have you when you were born, but your mom didn't let me." I questioned my mom about it when I heard this from my aunt for the first time.

I asked my mom in a mutilated manner, "You wanted to give me away when I was a little kid?"

And when I asked about this, she was astonished. She scrutinized my words and enquired, who said that to me.

I replied, "I know you guys have never loved me!" and to my dismay, I went off crying.

I have never had a talk about this to my parents because I was scared and reluctant to hear that I was a heavy sack of disgruntled wishes on them.

It's a sure thing that the reason my aunt wanted to have me was to help my parents to get rid of another daughter. My mom's brother was newly-married around the time of my birth and so they didn't have any baby and they were probably conferring succour in the times of need to my family.

At least, till I was some eight or ten years old, I was convinced with the fact that either I am adopted or my parents don't love me. Even when my parents have loved me beyond measures, given me the best of all possible things, I was never persuaded enough with their love.

My parents loved me, but I would never stop crying over the one time when I was scolded. But also, I'd never cry going to them, I'd always do it alone. Because I thought I was in a place that didn't really belong to me.

I tried to be one brave girl, who tried to be her own back. I tried to keep my pain to myself and not get any sympathy from anybody else.

The thought of being unwanted or adopted is the most haunting. Once it enters your mind, it just doesn't go away. It is indelible and it makes you relate every single happening of your life to this one thought. You'd build a mythological bridge which is not even pragmatic and your thoughts will make you keep walking on that bridge.

I didn't have many pictures from my childhood, which made this belief even stronger that there was some weird space between us. My mom had lost many of our pictures, she used to tell this whenever I asked her for more of my childhood pictures. And I would think of nothing, but one thing that they didn't want to make any efforts to hold on to my childhood memories because it wasn't as special to them.

Or maybe it was my mind that was creating stories to itself. Always over thinking!

Also, I've had the cutest baby brother after 3.5 years of my birth.

I don't remember anything unequivocal to that time, but I can summon up that moment when my grandma gave me a bunch of laddoos and asked me to go and give them to our neighbours.

Aha! They were celebrating!

And I had never seen that before. I could not think of the fact if my birth was celebrated too. But, it was a moment of happiness for me as well, but the sneaky `me' was actually jealous.

--

My father was born in a village of Punjab named,

Mukerian. He was a part of a big family. A family, that had eight children. My brother breaks his weird humour on this, saying, "You just missed three to have a cricket team at your home dad."

My dad was the youngest and naughtiest and a spoilt brat. He had been a troublemaker ever since he was a little kid.

He'd make the rest of his siblings get caught in the prank that he'd pull on them and would always sneak out of the sights of my grandpa, uncaught. He'd bunk school and would go for movies when all his siblings would go to school.

He is a chirpy soul, always giving belly laughs to the people who are around him. He'd spare no one, be it a little kid or a lady who is old to death.

If you are around him, you got to get ready to be vexed by his sarcasm. In all my twenty years, he has never scolded me like I've seen other parents doing. Nor has he done that to my siblings.

He will make you stand in front of him, repeat a whole damn history of your failures from your past in the most humorous way, say that you'd go highs. All these are his way of mortifying a person. He'd embarrass you to death without being rude to you even for a moment. Yes! I've got the coolest daddy.

Not only he excelled in entertaining, he was a quintessential man who catered his family with the best of everything. He always made his days and night meet to make sure that he's giving his children the best of the living. He has worked his fingers to the bone to provide his children the education that he bunked on. He has had left no stone unturned to make a dreamful living for his family.

My mother, on the other hand, was also born in Amritsar in Punjab.

She is the most generous soul and is almost the opposite of what my father is. She is not at all outspoken. She's always been into the spiritual world. She has been going to 'satsangs' (public gatherings to hear spiritual talks) since she was a young girl. She has always been all by herself. She had her own typing institute, where she used to teach a bunch of more than 150 students, which was a big digit to come across as a teacher at that time of past. She used to teach stenography and short-hand and was called 'lady villain' by everyone.

To her concatenation; she'd go to her institute, come back home, have dinner and hit right into the sacks without any loitering.

On weekends, she'd only go for satsang's. She was never into the world-talks and always lived in her own. My mom has never been into gossips and has always had zero interest in what society has to say.

And it is from her that I have inherited all of these characteristic traits.

My parents are all the way opposites and they do follow the law of attraction very well. They are one heck of a couple. Always strong and close! They are the one dreamy-perfect pair!

--

Childhood is a clay that can be moulded, it is the time when you make maxim' of memories for yourself, it is one of a time that doesn't come back and if your childhood didn't feed you with a silver spoon, that doesn't mean you can't feed yourself with a golden spoon when you grow up.

As a little kid, I thought I was what people thought of me. I was never an ecstatic spirit.

Being in India you are always going to feel the warmth of the heat that your relatives have for you. It's not always warmth of jealousy, sometimes it is the sheer love.

I've had a huge influence of my cousins on me when I was a little child. Most of them have been big bullies to me.

My maternal aunt used to make a visit of some 10 days every year from Punjab to Delhi. She had always been at our place during our summer vacations. Making plans to go for places during those vacations had been one of a kind.

But those times, too had a flip side for me. As a kid, those were the times of real hardships for me. My elder sister and my cousin sister would be in a pair, and my cousin brother and my younger brother used to be the other pair. And, I was always left alone.

My sisters would whisper words in ears and would laugh out loud together.

And it used to be heart rendering for me to have no partner to play with and I was always left in the middle of nowhere. It was like they always tried to put me to the ends. I could never be a part of their shenanigans.

My sister used to undergo a split of behaviour whenever my cousins would come over and it was even more hurting.

Even my cousins had never shown any desire of jellying up with me. It was like everyone always tried to put me away. I was never a pretty girl!

I had that brown tone that none of my close cousins really had. I was the only dark person or the 'darkest' person in the family and I had to hear jokes on that as well. I had a big nose and my dad would often say that my nose resembled to gudia. (the maid that we had at that time). He'd also say whether if I belonged to her. And this used to break me on the inside.

He used to come from his own fun space as he used to say all this, but that soft-hearted girl inside me was always at the verge of breaking. All these comments actually brought a lot of damage to my soul.

It always drained my confidence and made me believe that I was unwanted and not celebrated.

It made me believe that I had flaws, while nobody intended to hurt me, but I was always being hurt.

My second maternal aunt stayed in Delhi, she used to come over to our place every Sunday.

She too had a typing institute, where I was sent forcefully by my mom to go and study.

And I used to be very scared of her; it used to be nerve-wracking to have her at our place every other day. I'd hide in my room and would not even sneak out at the times when she used to be at our place.

I had another chunk of cousins across the street. I told you, family is a never-ending affair for Indians, the bigger it is, the better.

One of my paternal aunt lived just a street ahead. Along with my sister, I used to visit their house to play 'stapoo'. And there had never been a time when I had come-back without any lesion on my body.

I used to get hurt every time we played and I'd always come back saying they hurt me on purpose and I won't go to play with them again. But I always ended up going there again.

Not all days were dark for the little dark girl. She had one hell of a time doing crazy things with her siblings.

To start with the craziest moment of my childhood,

I remember that on a fine day, when I had just come back from school on a sunny afternoon. Both my siblings were back home too. And I've always had a strong intent to peek into the belongings of my sister. I was peeking in her school bag that day too, and there I got a hold of a sanitary pad and I didn't know what it was. I called up my brother and told him that she carries huggies to school.

And we couldn't fathom this weird fact. We were

curious to know what it was about. And the very same evening when our sister told our mom that she was going out to get a few things for herself; me and my brother followed her up all the way to find out if she was getting huggies for her.

And this is one of those freaky things that I've had done as a kid. And what makes my head laugh off today is that I involved my little brother to be another spy with me in this.

That's not all, me and my sister always made consistent efforts to make our brother do sister-ly things with us. We always involved him in our claptraps. He was a very cute little brother to have. I and my sister used to stand up on the big drums that we had in our backyard holding umbrellas. We'd make him shower water on us from a bucket with his hands and both of us used to usher in on some bollywood tracks. And that is something ludicrous to look back at now.

Also, another kooky incident that I can't hold back from sharing comes from a way back in 2005 when there was not too much buzz of computers in our area. None of my classmates had a computer at that time. And our dad bought us one.

We learned to access it all by our own, it was fun to play with that new toy. We'd spend hours in its lap. The first thing to do as we used to get back home was to switch it on and all three of us used to stay by its side till our dad used to come back home. And one day my dad's friend came over, he told us that we can't eat food by computers. He told us to stay away from it when we used to have our food. And that had such a formidable effect on us that none of us used to come nearby our computer whenever we were having food.

And this is so crazy and stupid when I look back at it and realise that how society had always made a way to crazy ideas that are to prevent the young minds from doing their things. Just to stop us from playing games on computer while having our food, we were made to believe in some strange fact. And that is not an issue at all. Issues are the one's which are fed to the brains of fledging generation that don't let them grow in their own world which is built by their own beliefs.

I had always been a rebel. I'd always cry and get the things I'd want to have. And my dad had never said a no for anything to any of us.

But, my elder sister never asked for things even when she wanted to have them and my younger brother never wanted to have much, so never asked for anything too. I had always been that one brat who'd have what she wanted to.

I have never been very demanding. I never wanted to have the most expensive toys to play with or the dresses to wear.

But, I always wanted to have things which were little, but everything to me.

I remember those flies that I used to have in my stomach the night before the day when I'd have to ask dad for the money for picnics. It used to be a constant beating of my heart with prayers to hear a 'yes' from him. And as a kid I wasn't really aware of the fact, whether if my father had enough money to give me or not, I always used to over think whether if I was asking for too much from him, but then I'd still not hold myself back from giving it a break and asking him for that.

And fortunately, he'd always end up saying a yes. Those were the moments that were over the top.

When I was that little girl, I had always been petrified of dad. For he had that French beard that scared me to death. I'd always get into my sacks before he used to get back home. I'd try to act like I was sleeping at the times when he used to get back and I couldn't really fall asleep.

I don't know what term shall I give to that feeling, but I used to try to hideaway for no specific reason.

I can't forget the summer afternoons, where he'd comeback during his lunchtime, and would stay home for some two hours. And every day, after he'd have his lunch and would be prepping up to fall asleep, he'd call me and say -"beta, thand pa de." (give me a warm hug) and I'd go to him, with my sneaky small steps, and would lay on his chest hugging him tight. And he'd hug me right back and give me a kiss on my head. And say some cute stuff and that moment used to say that this person loves you beyond measures, you silly little girl. And this legacy continued as to when I grew up my younger brother used to give those hugs to our dad.

On the other hand, my mother had always continued to serve us with her spiritual teachings. She'd take us to satsangs on Sundays whenever Maharaj Ji used to visit Delhi. I'd always cry because I always felt hostile towards bus travelling. That one month of the year when we had to go for satsangs used to be a woe ushered by long bus hours.

And once we used to reach there, my mom used to make us sit and listen to the complete hearing. And she'd say I'd ask what you've heard on our way back. And so, I'd just hear a couple of lines very fondly as to answer my mom when she'd ask us questions.

It used to get tedious to hear those long lectures on life. But then I was scared of God, and to me Maharaj Ji was my God. I thought that I'd be disappointing him if I won't pay attention to him. So, I used to attend those gatherings, sitting quietly, and always trying not to fall asleep.

And so, be it forcefully or by my own desire, I was always instigated towards the path of spirituality. I always believed in the name of lord. In that one power that was looking onto me always!

I remember sleeping on the left-most corner of my bed when we used to live in our old house. I used to have scary dreams and my mom would tell me to take name of the lord, be it in the name of any form of god. So as I used to lie in my bed, I'd keep reciting some holy mantra for 365 times counting on the digits of my fingers, following the paradigms of my mother. I'd do this every night before falling asleep.

If talked about my school days, I had always been a good student. I used to always hold some decent rank amongst top 4 students of my class till I was in the tenth grade. I was also a part of my school handball team. My mom used to tell my relatives that I was a good girl, she used to say that she never had to tell me to go and study or to do my homework; I always did that on my own and so did my younger brother. When it comes to studies, my elder sister had always crippled her way through. She had never been into studies and shit.

I got into a new high school after my tenth standard and that was the biggest turnover that I had in my life.

My previous school was not so rich. It was just at the end of the main street of my colony. It had decent environment and rules were not lenient over there. And my new school had completely different ambience, students over here were freaky and crazy. I had never heard so many slangs in my life as many as I heard on the very first day of my new school. Coming out of a colony-level secondary school into a so called international school was really disturbing.

Being brought into a whole new different environment, I could not manage to get along with this flip side. I could no longer digest the fact that 'I' was no longer the most called up student of the class.

Teachers did not even notice anything about me. There was hardly any sort of recognition of me. And because in my previous school I was the one who was most looked upon for all the activities and crucial events, it was not acceptable for me to go unrecognised like this all of a sudden.

I had never been used to such a situation where teachers called upon all their old, known students for their work and there was no count on me.

Also, I have never been a 'friendship' person. I've always talked to many, but cried with none. I've had friends which are no more friends to me as I grew up. The meaning of friendship changed for me over the years, and so I didn't make any friend because I could not find the people who were weird and shared a mindset like mine. I continued with none of my so called friendships from past. And here in my new school also, I didn't make any friends

And also, I didn't react well to the new situation, I wasn't actually able to be an astute, and make well out of that situation. I almost gave up on myself. I was no more interested in studies because I was not navigated well enough and for me, myself being a blind child, I could not make a way out of it. And in this fragile situation, I was made to swerve the flow of my thoughts.

As an outcome of this stressing situation, I was deviated towards the most talked of teenage syndrome-love!

And that was all I needed to get over this emptiness!

[2]
The princess found her way to glory!

* * *

'Sonali sharma'

36!

Exclaimed the maths teacher and broke the monotony of nervousness that was going inside me.

Not even 50 per cent? 36 out of 90! I talked to myself as I walked from my seat to the teachers table.

It's getting worse; I don't think I can deal with this. The conversation continued on my way back to my seat.

I didn't get up from my seat for the remaining four lectures and agitatedly waited for the school to get over.

36! The number kept hitting the walls of my mind

as I lifted my steps back to home.

Why can't I just do this? I can't do this, it's not for me.

The figure kept haunting me and I could not sum up the words that I would put forward to my mom as an explication of those numbers.

And when I reached home, I changed my uniform, washed my face and my hands without uttering a word, had my supper and went off to sleep.

As I walked towards my bed to fall asleep, I was hit by the question; just the one, that I didn't want to be asked!"What happened? Anything wrong?" my mom asked as she sensed my baited breath as I tried to steal a sleep to avoid any questions.

'No, I'm just tired.' I replied avoiding any sort of eye contact with her and pulled on my blanket and hit right into the sacks.

As I woke up in the evening, I gathered all the courage to tell my mom about how bad I had performed in my maths paper.

"Mom I've got the marks for my maths paper," I said.

"And...?" she added

"It's 36."

"Why so less?," she said after a 2 second glare at me; expecting a rational excuse from me.

"I don't know! I'm just not able to keep up with maths."

"But you'll have to. You have boards this year," she replied with elocution.

I had no reply to the conversation, and I was all clammed up.

"You can go for tuition, if you feel like you need it,"

she urged.

"It's okay, you don't have to worry much," she tried to boost me up at the same time.

And after all the toing and froing; it was decided that I'll be joining tuitions for maths from the falling week.

I've never had tuitions before that.

But I had to go there now!

I told my mom about the most talked tuition amongst my schoolmates, which was in my colony itself.

After enquiring on my own; I got admission there without any shilly-shally. My classes were scheduled on Monday-Wednesday-Friday, MWF, as they say.

Tuitions got started, maths got more of attention and this continued for the entire session.

School was going as usual. I was still the 'not into bad things' girl.

I was 15 and I was grown to 10 by now.

My mind knew of nothing, but only what my parents and my family taught me.

I talked to all the students of my class, I was the one who superintended almost all of the school events, I was called up by every teacher. Every student shared his problems with me.

I'd talk to all of them about all the issues, but not talk about 'stuff' to them; 'teenage stuff' is what I never talked about.

While all of my classmates talked about a lot of stuff and giggled at it. I always ensconced myself at the first bench; always talking to the teachers.

And maybe I did not even know what they were talking about at that time and it'd be a lie if I say I knew what they talked about.

They all were curious minds! Minds with curiosity for the things which were not to be talked aloud! And I was a "dumb-dead mind", I would call myself, because it was too late when I actually grew up, grew up to know about the things which were kept masked by society.

It was in my ninth standard when I heard the word 'sex' for the first time.

It was on page 52 of our social studies book.

Students in the class were advertising that before the lesson got started. It was a sort eagerness that was never before seen; they were never this elevated about studying a chapter.

It had to get started someday, And it finally got started.

Children were beatific this day. They were pointing out that one word, the word that held a lot of furtiveness. They giggled slowly as to avoid being noticed by the teacher. And I, had no urge to give any attention or any extra concern to that one single word that was very new to me.

I did not really ask any of them what that word meant and what made them laugh about it because I had no curiosity to know just another word (as it was to me) that was mentioned in the book. And for if it would have been something worth knowing, I waited for my teacher to explain it while he taught us the lesson.

And then, he read, the 'most talked about' line and then finally, the word of the day.

And the children were 'hee-hawing even more this time. The teacher continued with the explanation without really putting any emphasis on the word 'sex'. And when he noticed those giggles; he clarified sex means gender, whether you are a male or a female, it defines your sex.

And now, when I knew what sex meant, I could not understand what made them laugh about it. But I had always been consigned to oblivion; and it was easiest for me to steer clear of their talks.

When I was in the tenth standard, we used to have certain meets in our sports room which used to be only for girls! One of our female teachers used to address us in that gathering and a single section of students was called at once.

And she used to get started with her riddles that were never clear to me. She would spill the beans for us without really explaining the things she talked about.

"During your 'those' days, you have to make sure you come with proper breakfast. It's summer; carry some glucose water or some extra fruits along with your lunch to schools. You got to make sure that you are having proper diet so that you don't fall weak."

"Also make sure you keep extra sanitary pads in your bag always."

"And when using washrooms, make sure you abide those rules quoted over there inside your washrooms."

And her confidential tirade used to continue for the entire lecture and I used to be happy about getting a chance to skip our class and was never solicitous about what she talked about.

But one day; as I sat with a group of my girlmates, I asked them what does it mean. `Periods'?

"You really don't know?" said a girl in complete bewilderment.

"You haven't had your periods yet?" asked another one; in a diligent manner.

"No?" I said with a question mark look on my face as to know what was wrong about not having periods.

"What's it?" This time I became hysterical as I asked for an explanation.

"You bleed during your periods," one of them said and that was the most intimidating explanation to be given to a layman, I swear.

"What?" I asked in complete astonishment! Bleed?

How?

"Yes, your vagina undergoes bleeding during your periods."

And trust me that was the most frantic thing that I had heard in my life till then.

And while I was listening to them, just In the middle of that conversation, I felt some liquid dripping down my legs and my inner self screamed, "you are dead now" and I could not really believe that I had my periods just when I talked about it. I somehow, gathered all my courage to look down and see what ensued in that moment, I could see nothing and suddenly to my relief, I just saw water. Water! Water, it is I told myself and it was the biggest sense of solacity that I had.

The bottle that was lying in my lap was leaking and the water dripped out of it.

And it was the best news of the hour that I still didn't have my periods.

"How do you get to know that your periods have just hit in?" I questioned frightfully as to calm my nerves.

"You get to know that," they said.

"But, how? I mean what if they happen to me just when I am standing in the school assembly?"

"No, it doesn't happen that way, you don't have to worry so much. You'll get to know once you'll have them," they tried to fill me with aplomb.

Six months until I had them, I always worried about what will happen as to when they'll hit me for the first time.

But, you see I handled my first meeting with my periods quite proficiently and fortunately it wasn't in the school assembly.

- -

School was normal, tuitions were usual. There were duck faces in my tuition, but there were two guys, that I really noticed. One of them was strong silent type and the other was a impeccant and short.

They both were good friends and good entertainers for the whole batch.

The strong silent boy had a decent and quiet personality, while the impeccant one; Ironically! Was always at fault. He'd always do some mischief in between the class and would get caught and the onus would be on the taller one as well.

I really liked that silent guy.

And it was for the first time that I noticed any boy because I never really thought that one could like somebody without their parents telling them to do so.

I continued to have an eye over them during tuitions, but never really talked to them.

The short guy had a girlfriend, who was in our batch. She used to sit next to me and they both used to tittle-tattle over chats on phones in between the class.

I've never had a friend in school that had a boyfriend or girlfriend and this was really new to me. I confronted various things that were new to me by then.

And THE GIRLS GROUPCHATS!

Continued for a long, while in school and it became the wellspring of wild truths in my life.

Today, I was sitting in the 'girls group' and the topic for the day was SEX!

I asked them to tell me about sex. Yea, they were wiser and all the "don't talk about it" talks were their forte.

One girl with the maxim excitement broke the series of whispers and arguments to tell us that, 'sex is coming close to each other'; it's about loving, kissing, hugging and making love'.

"Ohhhh." I replied, while my mind was trying to perceive that explanation and it wasn't persuaded enough.

Because it appeared to be quotidian, and the meaning for the word 'sex' shouldn't have been normal.

They never talked about it openly, it must have got some deeper and nasty meaning to it. She's not really aware of the actual meaning. I ruminated within.

And another girl interrupted.

"No, you have to get naked when you have sex; and then you make love through body during sex."

"Whaatt?" Now this was the bullet to my head.

"Why would somebody get naked? How can they get naked in front of somebody?

What could be the reason of getting naked and holding the other person so close?"

But my questions would have accounted for my dumbness; so I rather preferred to keep all my questions to myself and replied 'okay' without any assertion.

And this was not it.

The conversation had a lasting effect on me. As I went home that day, I held my pillow close to me and tried to imagine some guy. I wanted to fill myself up with emotions that would make 'sex' sensible to me.

I tried to fantasise the moments that I would ever have with a guy in my life. And I thought of that strong silent guy in my tuition, but ended up thinking of that short guy. . I had no idea as to why it happened, but then I wasn't considerate about it at all.

The school was about to come to an end.

Tuitions were now over.

Boards were approaching.

.

.

And here they were!

My class 10 boards pitched up and I finished them off.

It was a long vacation that I had after the end of my secondary school and it was the time for me to head over to a high school.

As I told you, coming out of a colony-level secondary school into a so-called international high school was really disturbing.

I was indignant about not getting enough attention in my new school. But it was my decision to be there and I had no other option than keeping up with that new air. Even after completing my 10th grade, my thinking was not as open to erratic stuff as other children of my age had.

I'd come back home, depressed and exhausted not just because of my new school, but also because of the stress that physics and chemistry gave me. I was doing well in no place, neither in academics nor in the process of building relationships with the new companions.

I'd spend my time at home, sleeping or on Facebook. I did nothing productive and was being another sack of waste in the world.

Food-sleep-internet-and a disturbed mind was all I had.

It was just another day; when I had a friend request on Facebook from a guy that I had seen before.

Sin Malhotra, I opened the profile. It was the notorious guy from my maths coaching.

Ah, I know this person. And now, I knew his name too.

And the request was accepted.

And there was a series of elated emotions inside me after accepting the friend request.

It was about nothing, but I was amused and was looking forward to something that I could sense, was brewing.

It was 11:16 p.m. when I finally got a text from him.

And I replied like a whirl-wind without taking any time.

Sin : Hi
me: Hello
Sin : How are you?
me: I'm fine.
Sin : You are in which school.
me : tells her the school's name
Sin : Oh, I have my cousin there.
me: I see.
Sin : hmm.
me: :)
Sin : okay, it's late you shall be going off to sleep.
me : Yeah, I was about to.
Goodnight then. B'bye.
Sin : Good night, take care and bye.

And the first ever conversation ended. There was nothing invigorating in the entire conversation, but I still could not get over the friend request that I received from him and then having a conversation.

May be it was because I had noticed him at tuitions, so I was looking forward to our conversation. Or maybe the excitement was because I've had him in my dreams and I knew it was about to be something. That moment was enlivened by my intuitions that stipulated something that was on its way.

Next day in school, I was a little fidgety. I waited for school to get over and was desirous of heading back home.

And the moment I reached home, I galloped through my lunch in haste and plunged into my computer screen after having my meal. I logged into my Facebook account and found that there was no text from him.

And it was really a twinge to my expectations to see no message. I went off to sleep and told myself to comeback in the evening.

All my feelings and my emotions were drawn to that one person. There was some force that was dragging me towards him and I was beckoned towards a person in a way like never before.

I was in a fragile situation where everything seemed to be a boat to me. Desolation had struck me hard; no friends, new school and the arduous syllabus. It was all stressing.

I was looking for an escape and I thought of him to be my escape. MAYBE!

He looked like a perfect getaway at that moment.

I got up in the evening and went to my physics tuition and came back home.

I was on the tenterhooks as I wanted to have some affirmation for the intuition that was fostering within me.

I needed to hear from him and something that my heart wanted to hear.

I was waiting; waiting to be given a sly innuendo. I wanted to be given an allusion for the thing that my mind was already fancying upon.

'Hello', the text was finally there.

'Hi', I replied sprightly and waited for another half hour till I received the reply.

A decent conversation continued and he asked me, "So do you have a boyfriend?"

"No, but you have a girlfriend na?" I replied.

Him: No, we had a breakup.

Me : Why? I asked with curiosity.

Him : Just...

Me: It's okay, let's just leave.

Him : hmm.

Me : hmm.

Him : Why, don't you have a boyfriend?

Me : I've never had any.
Him : Why?
Me : Never found one.
Him : You never loved anyone?
Me : No.
Him : That's pretty cool, maybe it's the right time for a change! ;)
Me : :P not really!

It was 1 a.m. so I had to call it off! (Goodbyes were exchanged)

Our conversations were never over the top, but they still made me surmise my own mythical anecdote.

Same thing was repeated for a week until Sunday. When he asked,

"Will you be my girlfriend?"

It was not at all a fancy kind of a start. It started out of nowhere.

And I had no intimation about how I had to keep up the masquerade in that moment, but I tried to keep myself as a whole and not let my retarded emotions fall out.

"I need to think about it," I said. And made myself sound like a grown up, smart ass lady, who made no decisions in a hurry.

Next day on Facebook:
Him : So, what did you decide?
Me : Decide what?
Him : What I asked you about?
Me : I could not decide anything , I need time.
Him : So, how much of time do you need?
Me : Just tomorrow.

.

.

I was not really THE DAPPER LADY, but I acted like I was thinking of something sensible when every inch of me knew that I was thinking of nothing and I needed time for nothing because even with that time I could not think of things that I had never been on before. It was all new and it was for the first time that I was in the flush of a situation like this.

And because I did not know how I was anticipated to react; I tried to bring a delay to avoid ending up as a dumb-desperate bitch.

18th May 2013 on Facebook:

And I said a yes.

I had a boyfriend now.Phone numbers were exchanged

And now, I waited for him to call. He called up in the evening as he said he would.

And we talked about our families, schools, hobbies, likes, dislikes and everything.

Just not about the sun, moon, stars and silence.

It was a conversation for almost one hour.

-

-

We were 'young blood'.

Hap teenagers, who thought they were smart enough to make best of the decisions.

We were the real free spirits, who never worried about anything and just lived the moment.

.

.

School was tolerable now because he became the new thought inside the control unit of my brain. A lasting thought that subjugated all the bleak images.

It had been just 10 days since we had started talking and I was really indecisive about telling any of my classmates about it.

But I had to tell my sister! I had to tell her about the rare slate that I was writing on; I told her about the flying start of my relationship and she was pretty cool about it; she did not daunt me at all which made me believe that there was nothing wrong.

So the story began.

Our winsome conversations continued and I was perfectly distracted from my studies.

I was actually very happy about the new change and I deplored nothing.

.

.

And a part of me, wanted to be a doctor! As a medical student that's the only profession that you are told of and so was my mind told by me.

I never really looked at myself as a doctor, but then I was a medical student, so I had to be a doctor because when you are in such a milieu; you don't really have such a laissez-faire attitude for life. You don't get to think of being nothing, but a doctor as a medical student.

.

It was about to be a month and we had no meeting, but I was happy with the way our relationship was going. Although the only thing that ever ticked me was the fact that I was cheating on my parents by not giving attention to my studies.

But then I was happy about the new phase of my life and I didn't want to let it go at all. I decided to look on the silver lining that every cloud has and not to worry about the wrongs which were actually wrong.

Or may be the right thing to do was to give equal attention to my relationship and my studies.

But c'mon! It was my first love, how could I?

12th June, 2013.

1:15am

"Love" a word, I don't think my life is meant for, after all that's what it takes to be a doctor.

All these distractions have to be conquered,

But it's something that at least for once, should be enquired.

Well, one must enjoy every moment of life.

So I'll better enjoy the present and hope for a future with scissors and knife.

I hope this change will help me come out of the desolation.

But I'll make sure it doesn't become an obstacle in my preparation.

I can't say that I have any special feeling for you right now.

But I'm looking forward to see when it happens; where and how!

.

.

And the day had come, the day when we were intended to give a start to our rendezvous.

14th June 2013.

The day arrived!

The day for our first meeting.

I was nervous to my wits and I couldn't decide a way of retaliating on meeting him for the first time. I was trying to think of all the possible things that I might have to talk about.

I had never been out before."Out of my colony with my friends" and this time it was not just a friend, but a boyfriend. So I needed my sister with me. I convinced her to come along with us, so she was out there with me.

It was his birthday.

And I had to get him a gift.

I got him an archies watch and a card as the birthday gift. I urged my sister to bestow some financial aid on me.

It was for the first time in my life that I had hoarded some money to spend it on somebody other than me. And this was pertinent enough to testify the big and crazy deal that was happening right here.

.

We convened at the metro station and I just could not look straight at him. I couldn't clinch whether to say hi! Or to shake hands saying hello or if I should have given a greeting hug to him or maybe I was supposed to simply wave a hand saying hey.

I was left in another moment where I clasped close to my indecisiveness. But then, he made it easy by extending his hand forward for a handshake.

--

I was in a zone that I had never been into. I had all my tabs on. I looked after my hair for unnumbered times. I had a check on them for every single moment that I was spending with my boyfriend.

I tried to walk with more of elegance; I tried to give a decent smile and tried to make it look not too big. I made sure my face looked fine throughout the day.

I had never noticed myself as much as I did that day.

It was decided that we were going to watch a 5D movie "the lost world" first. As the movie began; everything was in motion there from our chairs to the screen, at least it felt like it was all drifty.

I've never had been a movie person, but it was whole another level of delirium inside me; it was because of that one person who was the reason behind all the anticipation inside me.

And a sensitizing thing happened; when our chairs moved! He just slowly moved his left hand over my right!

~And that was a thunder to my bones and a synapse to my breathe.

I've never had a guy other than my dad or my brothers touch me. And it was something I could not make out. I actually did not know as to what emotion I was supposed to draw out of that touch. I still don't know if I ever perceived right feelings out of it.

I had been so bad at putting right emotions at right place may be because I never watched movies or television shows.

I had nowhere seen people making romance and I had a complete cut-off from that because I was never allured towards such emotions.

But I knew 'somebody touched somebody' had to be a deep emotion and I tried to feel the intimacy of that touch which I was too immature to feel.

I did not look straight at him even for a single moment because that would have got all his attention focussed on me. And I didn't want that to happen because I was not poised about the way I looked. I didn't want him to lose the allurement towards me on our very first meeting because he did not find me pretty enough!

And to make sure that he stays, I tried to avoid any sort of eye contact.

.

And I avoided that eye contact forever. I was never assertive when it came to my looks. And it was disquieting to think of the fact that he might stop loving me if he noticed my scars.

--

But, I surely managed to notice all his little things that day.

.

His edgy and savvy shoes were at fleek, he had those perfectly coiffed hair.

Nails, perfectly trimmed on his cute short fingers.

Fragrance was enthralling enough to make me skip my breath.

.

And he had the prettiest smile that I had ever seen. He had those two deep dimples which were spellbinding enough for me. His fine and thin pink lips bloomed as he laughed.

It was captivating. His smile caught me. It was never before that I discerned somebody laughing that way.

But also nobody else had a smile like that. It talked to me in ways only I could apprehend. It said I want you to smile along. It said I'll take away your heart. It said I want you to come close to me and have a hold of me.

Everything about him was enough to make me feel the emotions that I had missed all my life.

He was surreal and he was a kind of water that tempted me to get into it even when I didn't know how to swim.

It tempted me to take a risk and just jump in.

Back to the movie?

I had my sister with me too!

And it's such a great feeling to have your elder sister out with you 'because that way; she's the one who pays for your food. While they both were making plans, I was there enjoying and fancying over my very first date with my boyfriend.'

He kept talking throughout the day and did not stop entertaining me and my sister even for a moment. We played games, laughed together and had best of the time.

He made me smile so hard and for so long!

He did that to me even when he was not really talking to me.

He worked magic on me.

He plated up my food for me, opened the soft drink can, brought me extra-tissues and did things that were perfect enough to make me feel like I was the luckiest person left on the planet.I was enjoying being pampered like never before.

The day was full of mirthful moments and was a perfect start to our journey!

"That best day!"

1:50 am

16th June, 2013.

Ah! Your birthday...

I think it was the best day...

Began with a pleasant meeting at a metro station, continued to a day full of exclamations!!

I had a smile on my face for the whole day,
And no wonder, it was really the best day.
"When we went for the movie,
You held my hand so tightly.
It was really a great feeling,
It was no less than a day dream."
The first meeting,
has really brought in some feelings.
I've started talking to myself,
And I keep thinking of you, just can't resist myself.

Everything was endurable now!

I used to be there in the moment physically, but my mind and my heart was always out there for him.

School lectures were tolerable; I would listen to the lectures while my mind used think of the things we talked of on the previous night.

It was the most beautiful thing that was happening to me right then and it was exactly the way I needed it to be.

I could call it a picture perfect phase because I had no picture in my mind for this before it started to happen. And whatever that was coming to me during this phase was something that I hadn't thought of, so it was eventually the best picture that was in continuation and was being painted as the things kept falling in!

It was about to turn into a two month relationship now and I made a bunch of friends that I talked to in school. School was also gratifying now. I told all my friends about my relationship.

They all were be smitten with our pictures that I used to upload on my Facebook. They all were in complete awe of us.

Anybody lionizing him, felt like, was praising me.

I'd start his topic in every period. I would tell them of what all we talked yesterday and and would just never stop. And they'd have to bear me for they had no other choice.

18th July, 2013
Written in biology period.
"Two months"
It's been two months now,
I didn't even realise how!!
Every day that passes by,
We have a lot of conversation, I always try!
There is nothing in this relationship that I want to change.
We will live together forever, I envisage!
I know I'm a bit too sentimental,
But, I think for a relationship, it's integral.
Well, whatever it is I'm satisfied.

Don't know about you as you've never told, but always denied.

You've really caught my heart and you drive me insane.

I want this to stay the same!

It was sudden start of a relationship with you and would go this much I never knew!

Love you!

.

.

Our relationship had best of everything, I loved getting mad at him for the most stupid reasons and he used to make me smile with his crazy and cute little things.

He cared about me in a way that was completely perfect and that was all I wanted.

He always tried to build a healthy relationship with everyone in my family. And he actually did!

He had been very much open about us and always sought suggestions from my sister and he played fun games with my younger brother.

He'd touch feet of my mom every time he'd meet her. And in no time, he became not just a friend, but a part of my family.

I too got friends with his elder sister, and we shared an amazing sisterly bond.

She'd complain about his younger brother to me and I'd feel so good about being his mother and listening complaints on his behalf.

And I'd later scold him and not talk to him.

And that was the best of all we had.

Overtime, our outings increased to forever and myriads.

And now, I didn't take my sister along with us for the movies.

6th August, 2013

Wave cinemas.

It was the day that was another best day to our bests. The best day kept changing as the days kept going forward.

And this was no ordinary day because what happened on this day was something that won't happen again, no matter what.

On this day!

I had my first kiss. First kiss with the love of my life.

We were sitting next to each other, holding hands. He slowly slid his fingers into mine as we watched the movie.

I would not lie, I was not there to watch the movie at all and I have never been out for movies, but to spend time with him.

And he always made my time, the best of the time.

He tangled his fingers from his right into the fingers of my left hand.

We both pretended as if we were watching movie. And we acted well. And it was within an infinitesimal amount of time his left hand was over my waist.

And what was it…

I could not keep myself into my senses. I was lost. Just a firm hold on my waist made me lose my sanity. I just laid my head back and pushed my chair a little back. And after a moment, that is exactly out of my mind, his lips were against mine as I came back to my senses.

And I closed my lips like anything and I didn't let him in.

I thought that was the way! I didn't open them and it felt like a door with lost keys

But my way; to me it was still the perfect one!

With his hands on my body, lips against mine what

I experienced was a blend of heaven with sins!

It was a mix of space with earth! It left a lightening in my bones and just shook my soul to its rock bottom.

It was the end, end of this life for me. It was delusive.

His hands moved around my waist and I was pulled towards him. I moved my fingers into his hair and he drew stars over my body. There was nobody around us. It felt like the entire hall was empty; half of it was empty because there were no viewers the other half was empty because we were completely lost in the moment to see anybody.

"Your heart is beating loud," he said as he brought his hand over my heart.

It eventually slid down to my breast.

It made no sense to me. I wasn't able to understand romance yet again. I wasn't even grown enough to have a pumped breast or I wasn't grown enough to wear bra, but spaghetti. But I had to keep up with the level of his romance so I acted as if I knew what all was happening.

Whatever was happening, his presence made me feel exotic. And it had the perfect finish to it. It was,

Lusty enough to draw me towards him and loving enough to keep me captivated.

It was the most extravagant moment, our souls were almost tangled and our breath mingled together and left us breathless.

Our hearts were beating like drums! Loud and wild!

A whimsical symphony was being played, straight from the heaven.

-

-

He loved me beyond measures, my heart always knew that but it was my mind that wanted to be assured at times.

But then he was perfect at answering all my questions with his touch. I could never stay mad at him for long. There had never been a single day when we didn't talk. No matter how mad I used to get; he knew exactly what he needed to do to make me laugh.

-

-

And it continued for our forever!

We'd go out for movies, we'd visit each other's place and we nurtured our relationship.

It never really had any valley it always got me high and higher.

I never had anything to complain about other than the one fact that he was not very expressive about his love.

I wanted him to blow a trumpet of our love to the world.

But we had everything our friends involved, our families too now!

Our families didn't know about our relationship, but knew us as good friends!

I was sorted and we were stable!

20th October, 2014

Oh! It's been so long now.
I know you are forever and wow.
I've gone all lame,
Have fallen in love so insane.
Sometimes, it gives me pain.
Tears shed out of my eyes like rain.
And I'm sorry for complaining again and again!
Thanks a lot for coming into my life,
And I just won't let you go without being your wife!
My love keeps growing day-by-day,
Throughout this life, I want you to stay.
Now, I find you like a piece of mine,

Without which the story of my life has got not even a single line.

Writing about you and your importance in my life,
Is the never ending poem of my life.

And I almost gave up on my studies because now, I had what I needed and I found no sense in focussing on anything other than him.

He was the only person I talked to. There was nobody else that I needed. And whenever he tried to tell me to have friends and go out with them as well; I always denied.

What I was experiencing during this journey was something that I have never even known before.

May be he also didn't know that how I was not out of my cocoon yet.

I was not really grown.

I was young love and stronger than anything.

My heart syncopated to its own lyrics.

May be my meaning for love was wrong or may be the love I was in was wrong.

-

-

We were done with our class twelve boards now.

And it had been a month and we didn't meet because of our twelfth board exams.

And so it was finally the time for us to meet,

We were having rough time in our relationship.

He had just started ignoring me and for me "he was angry".

Because maybe, I was irritating! I asked him for too much. I asked him for more of attention, I asked him to articulate his love into words. I wanted him to do nothing but love. May be my meaning for love was wrong.

Or maybe I was in the wrong love.

-

It had been two years now and our love was centuries old, it was strong and even keeled.

-

I had to meet him and apologise for asking for too much of love.

But this time, he was at the odds and was not ready to meet me for any business.

Because 'he was angry'. I told myself every time.

"I'm sorry, I'm never going to ask you for your time I know you were busy because of your exams and I stressed you even more. I'm sorry!" I said.

"No, I don't have to be in this," he said with refutation.

Yes, it was normal. We were not going to break up. He was just mad at me or maybe that was what I was telling myself. !

"You're angry. I know"," I repeated the same words on the phone throughout the conversation as to make myself believe that there was nothing wrong and he was just mad at me for getting into his interstices and not giving him his me time.

"Okay, I will wait, talk to me when you are okay,"I finally replied with the heaviest rock on my emotions and in the lowest timbre of my sound.

-

-

Two days and he didn't call. I was dead to death.

"You are angry I know, I am sorry," were the only lyrics to my song now. I reiterated this single line throughout the bijou moments of that long moment.

I was being signalled about how I'd be losing the love of my life in that moment.

But I believed in myself, my love was way too deep

to be shaken by the waves that retained on the surface.

His flip side was sudden but still not a shock; because to me, 'he was just angry'.

And love can get angry, but can never be gone. He needed his space, I tried to get out. At least, for a while now.

-

-

And I finally had a call after a few days.

Hello, it started...

And whatever he'd say would be because "he was angry", I told myself yet again, before it got started.

-

"I knew, you could not stay mad at me for long," I said to break the silence that prevailed after the hello.

"I don't feel for you anymore," he said.

He's extremely indignant now I enjoined within.

"Really don't feel like you are the one, I find something missing in this. I don't know what it is that I'm missing on, but my heart is not in peace, it craves for love but not your love. Not anymore."

He continued his one-sided verse while my heart was quavering and it chanted the melancholy of downcast.

"I know we haven't met since long and you are angry let's meet soon," I said. I had to speak something and everything to make him stop.

I could not speak much with my heavy heart which was drowning in its own deepness all of a sudden. The deepness that once held supremacy now brought sickliness. And my heart needed an escape from it in a trice.

"I don't have to meet you again. I don't feel that spark in us."

He spoke those heavy words with such an ease.

He was unaffected, but it stabbed right into my spirits straight onto the front.

None of us made a fake love.

The misreckoning was because our love was from different organs.

He loved from his mind and I loved from my heart. His mind was strong and my heart was weak. He could unlove the love, but there was no edit option in my heart.

We both had real feelings, but the strength of our realness was unmatchable.

"I feel for Vindi, she makes me feel good," so he was playing the loudest and the roughest beats on the drum of my heart.

But today, I was ready to take it all. I was ready to be beaten and not to be broken.

"Okay, I know I have always been jealous of her and you are trying to make me get mad so that I'd stop talking to you. But let me tell you it's not happening," I replied faking strong voice while I sobbed on the insides.

"No, I'm serious I adore being around her, I feel that warmth in her presence, I like her little things, I'm fascinated towards her. There's something that draws me to her." He thumped on the surface of my veins and arteries and made them stop to pump on the insides.

I almost lost my sanity now! I could no longer swim and I was almost drowning now. I was sinking into the water, a lot of water. One was the water of the flood that ran inside me and the other was the water of tears that rolled out of my eyes onto my cheeks.

It was all going wasted and there was nothing in the moment that could have saved me.

I know I am not pretty enough and I might not have a fair colour and the colours of my upper lip and my lower lip don't even match; also my gums are not pink and are oddly dark. My body might have pockmarks, but my heart is ostensibly not ugly. Can't you look at it even for once?

All this time, couldn't you ever notice how true and profound my love is?

I loved you with all my heart and it will never go!

"Love happens for one time and lasts for a life time"

So, you never loved me?

Or were you lying all this time?

You cannot cut the thin air all of a sudden and say that was not love; it was a dilemma that I need to get over now.

You can't do this.

And I know you are not even saying the truth, you are just trying to push me away.

So that I don't talk to you ever again.

I know you love me! What is it that is taking you back?

"I am not good enough for you! You did not do well in your studies! Just because of me.

I gotta go, so that you can have what you deserve, I'm too less for you! I'm of no proportion to your love! You deserve everything and I am nothing! I need to go," He uttered.

"Stop!"

"Stop lying to me! Tell me the truth?"

"Is it for some other girl? You can tell me! I just want you to be happy!

And you are my everything. There can be nothing better than this and you can't decide what's better for me"

I yelled, cried and I just wanted to be saved.

Why did you stay with me when you never loved me.

I know you are lying. Everything we had was not a lie It wasn't meant to be deleted. We can't erase feelings.

"You are angry," I said again I recapitulated this so

many times wishing that I could make my words turn into reality.

"You don't have to punish me so bad! I'm sorry, I will never repeat it! I won't complain!

You don't even have to talk to me for the whole day.

Stay! Please! Don't go," I begged.

Sobbing and skipping breath between the words.

There was no sound from the other end.

"Say something! I can't let go of you. I can't let go us.

We are perfect! There's nothing that we need to change.

Just stay, I will not be a cry child anymore; I just want you to stay by my side."

"Take care"

And he put the call on end.

I was numb! Water didn't stop coming out of my eyes. I tried to scream at the top of my lungs, but no voice came out. It felt like I had no voice left in me. I tried to hold on to invisible strings. But somebody had cut them down. I screamed out to the love of my life but my screams came back with the same speed, there was nobody at the other end.

I cried, cried for everything I had, it was being snatched away from me. I did all I could do to have that love by my side, I begged a little more to the demons.

"Please, let me keep this! I need it! That's the only seed of love that I planted in my life and you can't take it away when I have looked after it for all this time to make it grow into this big tree!

You can't do this! You are not just popping out that one tree from its root, you are taking a part of me away with it! You should have not let it grow if you wanted to take it away!

It's too late; I won't let you have it back now! It's

mine."

I cried and negated the decision that was being made by demons. I was skipping breaths, I was getting numb, I threw my hands in exhaustion and I was falling, falling down from my terrace. The wind almost slapped on my cheeks. My heart pumped even louder and stopped all of a sudden.

.

.

IT WAS OVER!!!!!

MY BAD DREAM!!

Bad enough to haunt me to death. It shook my heart deep till its substratum!

It made me cripple in that moment.

It was not for real; it was just a bad dream. I told myself, it was over.

It might have been as long as two years, but it was just a dream and I collected myself to put my parts to their right places.

I could breathe now, in the new air. In this air, the only scent that lingered was of my thoughts. Thoughts, that were stronger and were having all marbles.

It was such a sense of relief to know that it was just a dream and it was over and now and this time I was equipped enough to back up myself to have a life which had no shadow of that crazy dream.

I learned everything! Everything that it had to tell me!

It told me, how deep I could love somebody.

It told me that I had the tendency of going beyond limits for somebody.

It told me, that within my body, there was a soul that could not get naked to everybody!

It told me, I was too beautiful to be loved by someone ordinary.

.

It seemed to be perfect and everything that I needed, but I could not see what woes it had to spill on me.

It was treacherous, mysterious, agonizing yet everything that I wanted. It made me feel bad about myself because I could not convince someone to look at me the way I looked at them. It made me put myself in the worst phrases. I thought that if it'd get over ever! I'd lose my existence too.

It was my mind that was never making good stories for me. It always made continuous reminders of my wretched attributes. And till the time I was stuck in that moment I was never really able to get into a rousing space that was really waiting for me out there.

A space that had all the good things in its stock for me. All this time, I was doing nothing but keeping myself away from the things that I really deserved for the things that looked good to me in that particular moment.

It was all gone, but it filled my mind with more words; my heart with more emotions and my life with a lesson.

He came,
Came to tell her how to love and let go.
He came,
Came to tell her you'd come across millions on the go.
He came,
Came to tell her not to hold on to the things so easily,
He came,
Came to tell her you are b'ful, you silly.
He came,

Came to tell her how it felt to cross miles for another.

He came,
Came to tell her be your own first lover.
She was so much of innocence,
She was infant in her adolescence.
She couldn't stop new things from pourin' in,
She knew nothing, but was just trippin'.
Deep into something which was concrete,
She never gave up, for she had enigma & was an athlete.
She was an ocean while he was just a drop,
He was a barren land where she tried to crop.
She was the book for if he was a page,
She was thunder with unsippable rage.
She was the destination if he was a path,
She was left always into rath.
She was the feeling if he was a poem,
To his endings, she was proem.
She was always beyond the measures.

When life happened, I was brought back to the drawing board, so that I could redraw the picture for me, and this time I could embrace those scars; with all the lessons that I learned, I was wiser. I was stronger and above all I learned to accept me for myself.

Whatever it was, it was the happiest moment at that point of time. But when it was gone, it left me with the best version of me. It helped me grow! Grow into the real sassy bitch that almost lost its existence. Bitch that was worth it all and was still trying to hide!

I could now, look over things in a new way. I had new visions to life. I was made to come across the most alluring aspects of life. I was now ready to accept that sometimes, even if you give your best, things are not going to fall into your way as you want because it's not meant to be.

I had spent two years in the name of one person; I got so lost into that moment that I gave up my own identity. But, as to when it got over! It gave me an outrageous scintilla that never went off.

It brought me to my real grounds. I was not ready to have this new start but when I stepped forth, I realised why it happened. And ever since then, I could never stop appreciating the decisions that god had to make for me. His decisions were nerve wracking, they were not the yummiest at times, but still they were the best ones!

She was going to hold on,
She was going to hold on, not to him but to the lessons she learned,
It became mere past on which she once yearned.
It was her most reminisced melancholy,
It was enough to leave her nerves in alcoholy.
He went,
Went to leave her stronger than ever.
He went,
Went to make her go albatraoz forever.
He went,
Went to tell her she was magnificent.
He went,
Went to tell her that he was not sufficient.
He went,
Went to make her know herself.
He went,
Went to let her create a new self.
She carried it,
She carried it wherever she went,
She was broken but not bent.
She carried it in her brain right before her heart,
It was dead matter which she carried like peart.

She carried it not to forget it ever,

She knew that it was over, but it was the best lesson ever.

This ONE incident not only changed the way I thought about myself, but also about my endeared ones. I learned to appreciate the love of my parents that often seemed bogus to me. I learned to value their unconditional love that was showered on me even when I was always complaining.

Once getting hurt for my love being unnoticed, I realised that I should have given more value to my own kith and kins instead. Even though I have always loved them beyond measures, but what I felt now was alarming.

Every situation can be dealt in two ways, you can either look onto its positive side or you can look at the negative one. And your pick in the situation is decided by the kind of beliefs you have.

This situation was heartbreaking and was hurting enough to leave me broke; I was completely bent out of shape.

But I had a choice; I could cry the blues or I could turn the blues to marvellous violets.

At the onset of it I was numb. I could not figure out what happened. I tried to deduce all I could from that one heartbreak.

I knew that I gave my all in that situation, and for if it didn't end up the way I wanted it to; this simply meant that it had to teach me something that couldn't have been taught in any other way.

I was able to rise instead of getting into the dumps because I chose to look at the bright side of the situation; not even for a single moment I doubted the power that owns me!

I might have doubted myself for not being good

enough, but when I confronted the hardest knockdown in my life, I realised that I was living on a whole wrong rebel. I could now understand that I was put in one hard situation so that I'd have my eyes open to celebrate the better moments of my life.

I had a broader and a wiser vision to everything in my life! I learned to extol instead of criticizing the verses that life played on!

TINY?

Ahan! I see you there my boi.

So you remember? The one thing that I talked about when I started introducing myself to you, the thought of being an adopted and an unwanted child?

Yes! That thought did go away! And nobody but my own mind helped me to let go of that thought!

Over time when I saw that I was given everything that I asked for, I started appreciating those things. I no longer stood by my ideology of being unwanted when I decided to feel blessed about the things that were given to me and not taken away from me.

I realised that I could make it either way, I could either convince myself that I am unwanted or I could tell myself that I am loved!

In whatever way I convinced myself, the outcome was contoured with the filter of my suggestion only.

I learned that we could really decide the way we want to look at the things, we can apply a particular filter to our brain and we'll get to see everything around us with that particular filter itself!

And this thing is a real proven fact!

If you keep reiterating a thought that you don't like a person then there is no way that you will be able to love that person. No matter how good that person will do to you, you won't be able to look at their benevolence till the time you don't let go of that filter that you have just applied in your mind for that person.

And if you have faith in a person, you are going to trust that person even if that person ends up cheating on you. And this is because you have applied a filter of faith and trust for that person and no matter what that person is doing you're going to look at him with that filter of faith!

So you get it, why you trust your partner even when you are cheated by them time and again?

It's because of your filter of love and faith TINY!

And this is how these filters are working in our lives.

If you apply that 'I can't do it' filter to your mind then in no way you're going to make that happen!!

And with a 'I will make it happen' filter you'll end up doing things which you might have given up on without that optimistic filter.

These filters let you go forth with a particular belief! The beliefs in these filters are strong! They occupy a space in your mind and take a huge control over your reaction to the situations that you are put in.

So next time if you are dealing with any situation, make sure that your filters are vivid! Don't let your life get dull with a wrong choice of filter!

And when you have been given choice of making your pick then I find no reason of making a not-so-hap choice!

As I healed from the lesions from my past, time came when I had to head for college; I was quite groomed by now to handle the forthcoming situations in life.

It was the time when I made another decision for myself. I decided to opt for Bsc. (H) Forensic Science to get my graduation degree.

I was into new spirits and I was looking for doing

well in academics this time. I believed it was the high time that I payback for those huge bucks that were spent on me for my high school-ing and I ended up wasting them.

It was in the month of July when I went to look for a college that Google marked as a leading college of India; it persuaded me enough to go and check it out.

It was a far-fedged college in Greater Noida. And it took a three hours journey to reach there. And a three hour journey to the way back to my home.

And after all the chewing of fat,

I got my admission in that one college and I was now waiting for it to get started, it started off way late than usual.

It was on September 13, that we had our orientation.

And then it started, a new journey of my life. It was Thursday when I had my first day in the college. It was far cry from the regular days. I had countless people around me from all the races of society. I had never heard from people from so many different states of India under one roof.

The thought that I'd get to live a new life was ravishing. I was very keen to find out what was next in the casket of life.

I talked to a lot of people on the very first day. I didn't want to feel out of the box this time, so I decided to take initiatives by myself.

I decided to be strong and handle the new environment with grace. It was the second day when I talked to a few more people and asked them where they were staying and out of all the 100 people 90 were the ones who stayed in hostels or PG. And again, I was under the influence, influence of society.

Everyone around me said that it was not possible to travel for six hours and keep up with the studies. Their talks swayed my decision yet again!

I got back home on Friday and made yet another declaration that I won't be going to college via metro anymore since it's not possible. I told my parents that there is not even a single child in my class who travels this long.

I was told by my parents that it was my own decision to go for such a remote place! But I chewed the rag alone, without listening to them and just being robust about my decision like always!

And like any other time, this time also my father agreed!

It was a Saturday when I called up a girl from my college to send me pictures of her PG; I showed them to my dad and packed up my luggage so as to move in that place by Sunday. Everything was done in a hurry.

Because being patient was not in my script.

Never in my life had I thought of going away from my home. I remember when I was a little girl, I used to keep my mama's picture in my bag. And when I used to visit my grandma's home, I'd look at that picture and cry at night because I used to miss my mom. And this sudden plan of moving out of my family was capricious.

I lived in PG for a month and then moved in to a flat with my seniors. I used to come back home every weekend.

My mom, had shown her full-blown love during this time. She'd keep stuff for me that I could take along with me to my place. My siblings would complain about how she was being partial and giving me preponderance.

It was every week that I visited my home, but it was always that my mother's eyes would go wet whenever I used to hug her to bid good-bye. Those were the times when I could feel the depth of love that was there in her heart for me. She always did little things to make me feel more special.

I was always asked if I needed something'. I was given everything' I could ask for. And being alone there I learned a lot! I learned more about the love that my family had for me.

I started to look over life in all the rarest ways. I was able to find good in every situation. The way I thought was even more altered now!

My relationship with people changed! I remember how that time helped me to sort out the ego-issues that came between us 'kids' and our 'maternal aunts'. I also worked upon the equation that we had with our cousins.

I worked on everything that I thought was going in a way that was wrong.

I talked to myself that about how,

I have met a broke person and a happy person. A person who's always helping others and the other who's not really bothered about others. I've met a secluded person and a loud person. A person who was kind and another who was bound to his highness. A person who is content and another who is always wishing for more. But none of them was a bad person; they all had a good heart!

It was their reaction to a particular set of circumstances that made them different and we misconstrued their reaction to be them! These attributes were mere reactions which we discern as their identity.

It was just after four months that I thought I was evolving! I wanted to learn more about life. And I decided to get back home! For it was the society that made me feel that I could not go for a 6 hours travelling and then keep up with my studies.

And so, the rebellion me wanted to disprove them this time!

It was a series of emotions that I was running on!

And that movement was constant; there was a gear up in my race over time.

I came back home and started travelling for six hours to get to the college and make a way back home. It was the same thing that I was doing that I once told my mind I couldn't do.

A six hour travel, back and forth to college might not sound like an achievement; but to me it actually was! It brought a lot to my life.

And what I learned out of this was another biggest lesson of my life!

I learned that;

Everything that we are telling our mind, is going to happen. What we feed our mind with, is what it is going to grow out for us.

Society is always going to make us doubt our potentials. It is always going to convince that things are difficult and it is up to us that how hard we want to make it happen. For if our desire to get something is strong then no person in this world can stop us from making hard things happen easily.

I continued to travel for 6 hours every day! And those six hours of my day were the only hours that made me what I am today! I won't lie that these hours were spent to go to college, but I didn't have any steadfast studies once again this time! I used this time on my self-growth instead.

I created bundles of thoughts, some were meaningless and some were everything!

I'd keep listening to music all the way in metro and make pictures in my brains! Pictures to my perfect life.

I'd observe people around me! I'd notice how some of them were happy with the little things they had and how some were complaining in spite of all the expensive possessions they owned.

As I'd sit in bus after metro I'd look out of the window onto the dreamy skies! I'd notice how the skies had a perfect mixing of all the shades of blue. I'd notice the speed, the air, and the trees and would think of life!

Hey TINY!

I know you must be wondering what I thought about life!

I thought of how this life was working out for all of us. I discovered that a power had control over me.

--

I recalled all of those childhood moments and the memories where I used to think of the things I'll be doing as to when I'll grow up.

Little things like getting a new haircut and then getting my hair turn red in colour. I always used to make a picture of the things in my mind before they'd actually happen in my life.

I painted that picture of a new high school and got into one as I wanted! I thought of one college and got into the one I wanted.

I wanted to get inked and always managed to get my new tattoo by the date I'd decide!

I'd go to trips alone all by myself whenever I wanted!

I always managed to do everything that I wanted and this was may be because I believed in myself.

Even if it was for the tinniest things but I never doubted my powers.

I knew the almighty that owns me, was always there to give me things that I wanted in return of the unshakable faith that I've always had in it.

I never settled till I got things I wanted, I was ready to have the bitterness of the struggle to have the intimidating taste of the victory.

These things might have been mere happenings but to me they are a reason that made my belief stronger in that power that has always helped me to make my mark, just the way I've ever wanted! These small achievements pushed me to go forward to try and have a bigger bite from the cake of life.

That power was like some force that always confined me! It always guided me to me to deal with the worldly goods.

What made me believe in the fact that there is some power that is controlling me; is the fact that there were the times when I was gridlocked from doing things that I was really willing to do!

And if there would have been no force that was controlling me, I wouldn't have been stopped from doing the things on my list.

I believe that I have got some attributes of spirituality because of all the beliefs that my mother had.

She had this one invocation of predicting things in her life and getting everything she asked for! And I got this too as a benediction from her.

And eventually, I too got into a spiritual world that was created on my own! I still don't have any picture to my power. I don't know about its geometrical figure but what I know of is its vibes. I know of the small gestures that it keeps giving me.

This one rare thing has helped me to have almost everything in my life. It helped me to solve most of the equations of my life. It told me that how I am that one blessed creature that was sent to earth. It gave me so many reasons for my existence.

Travelling helped me to see good in people! It helped me to know them without even talking to them for real, I learned to share smiles for no reason! There were times when I ended up talking to rarest people in the rarest moments as I travelled my way from home to college and back.

Sometimes, it was just a share of glance, sometimes, it was just a share of smiles and there were moments when conversations started from giving a small space to sit and ended as sharing of life stories with that person!

I talked to a lot of strangers but never saw them again! It was fun to talk to so many different souls and end up knowing about their life thoughts! I used every individual as a brick in the wall of my life! I made continuous efforts of learning; learning about what life means to other people.

Sometimes I'd just compliment a girl for her hair, another for her eyes and to somebody else I'd simply say you look pretty! Or 'You have a great smile', to a few and getting that XL smile back used to be heart-warming!

Trust me, if you'll start spreading love, your stock will keep increasing and you'll love to share it even more!

As I travelled my way through this life I could find out that we could actually talk to those powers;

Those powers are out there in countless forms and none of us is wrong in believing in any of the forms to be our god!

Over time I began to relate all the contingencies of my life to this power. I began to believe that power is always giving me some gestures at every instant of time. And I was able to sense them sometimes but not always.

I could not really find out a way of interacting directly to that power. But then there were sometimes when I wanted to hear answers from that power and I used to get the answers from the digits in the time!

Yea, that's how I interacted with the 'power'.

I'd think of a question in my mind and would look

at the time in the clock; whenever it used to be an even number the answer used to be a 'yes' and an odd number was a 'no'.

I tried this over a month as to see how a 'yes' actually happened to be true and a 'no' stopped things from happening in reality! Power was actually answering me!

Now, it might not have been the power that was giving me the answers but my belief said so! And I made my belief so strong that there was no other way how things could happen for me!

I could actually feel like I was able to control a lot of things in my life; I used the digital medium to interact with the power!

Believing in my invisible powers was fun! I would play some music in my headphones and would keep thinking of every aspect of life as I had that six hour journey.

I'd think of myself without relating me to others. I'd treat myself as the only centre to my story and would try to untangle the knots that made me get attached to the things of life that surrounded me.

As I began to detach myself from the strings of the society, my connection with that power got stronger.

I would silently think of all the questions that would strike my mind and I would answer them for myself.

And this was my form of meditation.

I realised that there doesn't have to be a way of meditating and taking the name of lord! We could do it any way and anywhere.

Meditation, to me is about setting your soul on peace! Setting it free from thoughts of the society and concentrating on one power that you believe in.

You can talk to that power all day long, it's listening. But it gives it'll respond only when it's required. And that response usually remains unnoticed because we are not fully aware of it.

And for if you start believing in it you end up having answers to most of the question that you'd have about this life! You can give a shape to that power, you can create a picture for that power or you can simply say that it lies in a person! You can believe that your power is your parents or your grandparents.

I could have named that power as any of the godly images that we have been told about but that would have meant going by something that wasn't uncovered by me on my own.

Whatever you believe in! Your belief should be stone thick and shall be unshakable. And once you start believing in that power you'll always end up with all your problems getting solved and you'll find solutions to your problems even at your wits' end!

Because with a strong faith in something you don't get ready to give up till things happen your way. And maybe that's what makes you believe that the power worked for you when it's you who's actually doing things!

Ah, my tiny boii,

I see you getting all pissed over there; cause of these spiritual talks now!

You don't have to get mad anymore, I've got even better crap to talk about!

Fascinating crap you know?

Come over!

EXPLICIT CONTENT LIES AHEAD !!

[3]

The crap trap!

* * *

For the times I was told that I'll have to cover my body to be at a holy place, my inner self would say, "They are crazy", because seeing people judge others for their clothes even at temples is obnoxious!

I can't believe that you have grown up in any way if you still point out such things even when you are following the path of spirituality! The path of spirituality is not related to the language, colour or the manner in which one presents himself to that power!

It is completely dependent on the faith! It's about working on the inner connection and not on the outer world.

~People would give you definitions of god! They'll

tell you about religions and it's a kind of trap that they are in! And they are just increasing the count of people who are caught up in that trap with them! They try to involve more people into this!

You don't have to hear no one! You've got to decide everything on your own. You got to find out if you really feel any power that is actually within you.

Or do you feel a power which is kind of superintending you and is a well-wisher of yours?

It is there, and it is up to you to decide the way you want to look at it! You can completely ignore it or you can blindly believe in it!

If you will go with the way that has been set by the society, you'll have to abide their norms!

They'll tell you that `you can't do this' when you are addressing your power and `you shall be doing that' to worship your god!

But you my boi can do anything till the time your inner consciousness doesn't say that you are doing anything wrong! And if it doesn't you can climb up any tree and anyhow!

~They'll tell you! and you got to untell them!~

TINY!

I want to ask this to you as well if you agree with this society.

What makes you say that you can't scream 'fuck you' at a temple?

For if god doesn't want you to say that he can cut your tongue off! He won't let you speak anything that's inapt.

All these words and clothes are no measure to show respect to someone!

Only measure is our thinking and untaintedness of our spirit. If we have that purity in our soul and clarity in our mind; we are going in right way of worshipping that power!

And if our thoughts are sinful and our soul is not pure then there is no way that can get us to that almighty!

It was us who made languages, it was who made these clothes. And it is us who are spreading these fabricated thoughts.

It's not god who's using these shrewd delineations but it's us who are doing it!

What they say is right but how they are implementing it is getting wrong at times!

~They are trying to get out of the trap of the 'moh-maya' but are still stuck in it! No matter how spiritual their talks are they are still judging people at 'sat-sangs' for if they wear some short clothes or use some slang words.~

No I don't want to wear any short clothes to holy places but I want not to be judged when I end up going in those shorts there someday! Because I know my lord is not judging me! Then why do these people have to complicate it for other person?

When in this life are we going to stop bothering people with our thoughts?

~When can I not worry about my head-scarf and just interact with that almighty?

When can I bow down infront of the lord at the temples without worrying if my jeans has slipped down and my undies are showing up?~

And every time I talk of wearing less or no clothes, it's not because I want people to go around naked. They look b'ful when covered! But what I want is that we give no puffery to someone who does that!

And if you don't agree with me at these points then agree or not! The society has got the control of you as well!

And you have given no individuality to your thoughts!

~I hope that someday, we'll go to the temples, just to worship our god and not to be judged!~

And when we are talking already! I want to talk some more!

It is another rebel that I want to get out of my head.

Why are we giving this non-required attention to this four lettered word FUCK? When it means nothing but having sex!

Sex helps us to produce life and make love! What could be more b'ful than that?

Why are we giving this discretionary attention to the breast and the penis?

We always tried not to have birds and the bees kind of talk casually! We try to hide such things and that is what makes people to use this minutiae as a weapon.

Why are we letting others think of abusing others this way?"

~The society is making us think that vagina or the penis hold any value, value of bullying others. We are able to harass others sexually or mentally through these things only because we have given these things unnecessary attention.~

~When are we going to make it look all-okay to us! When is it going to be a no big deal to talk of breasts and penis publically?~

For if our thinking would have been sober! No one would have thought that fucking someone could be a source of pain to their psyche.

No one would have thought of raping someone to cause some trouble in their life, because if fucking would have been about just making love, a rape could have never caused any harm to a girl! It just could not ruin her life!

~The things that are kept secret and are talked

slowly often lead to results that are loud!~

And this is one of the reasons why we end up in such situations!

For if we'd have sensitized our kids about this on our own, they wouldn't have ended up giving a bad meaning to it!

~Our minds are wasted! And we got to change them before it's too late!~

And not all of our minds are wasted some are just influenced.

We are making this dirty business become 'the greatest business'!

Nothing but the vulgarity of our thoughts is becoming the fuel to this business. If we would have been open about the things we call 'non-veg' , they could not have been 'non-veg' for any time longer.

~We are beeping the slang words in a movie and increasing the curiosity of the young minds!

This way, we are not preventing them from thinking about "bad things" we are tempting them instead!

We're making them give a bad meaning to it.~

Early man, was not equipped enough to know about the art of clothing; it was late after the Stone Age that human invented the 'art of clothing'. Until then there were no clothes and with evolution, our ancestors first covered themselves with leaves and later on, the fabric clothes were brought in effect.

Naked, then covered with leaves and finally fabric clothes!!

~Ever heard about the rape of a naked man? Or the one that was covered with leaves?

Not really!

It's not the size of clothes that is causing troubles but it's the size of our mentality that is causing troubles!~

~The solution is not to get naked bodies but to get naked minds.~

Naked minds are the minds that need to be free from vulgarity! We need to stop giving weightiness to the things which are nothing but mere organs.

I would no longer waste my time on talking about them views but the good things that we can do for ourselves!

It's okay to feel bad about the way the society is not growing.

But guess what? We can just cut them out of our world! We can have a world of our own without any judgements and low-levelled criteria's that are set by the society!

It's not that all of us are in that trap! you gotta trust me, there are some b'ful souls out there which are actually doing well in their lives. Which are actually working on the good's of their lives instead of caring about what others have to say!

While some are still struggling their way out of the trap of society.

And the best part is you can decide if you want to stay in the trap or come out of it!

TINY?

I want you to feel okay if you are not okay with their thoughts! I want you to be happy that your thoughts are distinct to society.

I want you to raise your voice and say no, at the times when you don't agree with them!

Let us together build a new society!

~A half naked woman or a completely naked man no one should be treated, treated with no judgements!~

~I don't want you to mould yourself to fit in their criteria's; they'd make you lose your worth! Make sure you don't get cropped, cause you are worth growing my child!~

~So keep growin' in your wilds! ~

And before you dig deeper pits with me, here are ten things that you need to read…

10 THINGS YOU DON'T HAVE TO FORGET!

1. "You are strong beyond measures", everything that you need to be is veiled with your body.
2. You are an "individual" and nobody else can decide the way you live your life. Don't let others influence you in any way. Don't you get deviated from your path because somebody told you that the other one is a short-cut. Don't let them tell you what's better! You got to decide on your own how you want to crumble your cookies.
3. You can achieve your goal only if you are ready to work for it! You can't have your bit as you sit! You got to stand and run errand! You'll have to pay the price for the things you dream of!
4. "Uncertainty" will strike on you at any moment! And you don't have to get spent. You got to keep your back up and stand by yourself! Because these uncertain situations end up leading us to the most felicitous junctures in our lives.
5. "It might be a dark day, but never a dark life", and you can be the lamp of that dark day! You just have to know that it is the time which is not going to last forever and you have to know it'll guide you to the lights as you'll go ahead!
6. You can't blame others for your damp squib, you need to know that you lacked efforts when you are made to face a defeat! You need to get your shit together and get back at it again! You need to be stronger than you were last time. And you need to make your efforts be suffi-

cient enough to have that last straw!

7. If you have given up! Then there is no way that you can make it! Miracles happen only when you let them happen! And if you are not letting them to happen to you then you are just limiting your life to the grievance. "If you believe you are sad then there is no way that you can be happy!"
8. "As strong as your belief as strong will be its possibility of happening for real", eventually you'll end up with your beliefs turning into reality if you have believed in them indomitably.
9. Your life is a treasure that has innumerable mysteries; you need to be ready to believe that you are going to encounter the most flabbergasting facts about life only if you'll try to find them out. "You just don't have to let go of this life in vain, you got to get into its deepness to see magic."
10. "You are just a creation". A creation of an almighty power, a power that owns us! Our creator is always eyed up on us and is always sitting there quietly throughout our happy days to the days of doom! That power is always alluding about what is going to come next! But only if we are at that level of consciousness then only we can figure out these gestures.

[4]
There's a you & there's a me

* * *

So?

Wake up!

Tiny boi, I got to ask you something again!

Who do you think you are?

What do you think you are made of?

What do you think is the reason of your existence?

I want you to take a spell to answer these questions for no one but yourself.

These questions may not be the most intriguing ones but they are worth it all!

They are worth it to make you know a li'l better about the life that you are living.

And before I break it all to you I want you to get answers for these questions.

YOU CAN HAVE YOUR TIME!

I don't know how much you have got to know about "you" but I must tell you about "me".

And Imma tell ya not just about my "me" but your "me" too.

So tell me do you feel that 'me' that's inside of you?

Do you ever feel a voice that keeps hitting your mind day in and day out? Do you feel that there is a system within you that is producing stimulus to the world that lies outside?

Now tell me how much of attention have you given to that voice that's trying to get promulgated?

Or tell me what kind of voice is it? Is it telling you that you are good enough to live this life or is telling you that you are having short of any beauty?

~Yes! Your' me' keeps making storybooks for you. And till the time you don't decide what kind of story you want it to be! It'll keep creating a story on its own!~

Yes!! You can decide your story. Your 'me' can be just you, it can be the real you which is not suborned by the society or anybody else.

Most of us are feeling sad about the life we are living because our 'me' is not happy with itself! It feels that it isn't good enough to make a killing in the world which is souped up!

You got to tell your 'me'!

You got to tell it that it is perfect and it doesn't have to think that it isn't good enough!!

What I am saying is that if you will not get this thing in your sub consciousness that you are everything that you need to be and then you will not be able to feel good about yourself.

You don't have to think of all those people who are telling you that you are not good enough. 'What you have to think of is yourself and all by yourself.'

~Don't let people tell you that you are what?

Tell yourself that I am this!~

~Because till the time your thoughts are not saying that you are a star you can't manage to shine on the outsides!~

You got to love your scars and embrace them. You have to love them for yourself and not to prove anything to others.

You don't have to be weak! For if you are weak, you can't deal with the heavy cannonade that life bombard onto you!

You have to keep telling yourself that you are good enough! You don't have to think that you are fat, skinny, short, tall, dark, fair, this or that! All you have to think is that I love myself! You have to know that you are perfectly enough to live this life by being your own self!

~For if you tryna change yourself, then you are losing that 'me'! You are no more 'me' if you are trying to change yourself to set in the framework of the society, for if you're doing that then you are actually losing your own psyche.~

~You are an art! An art that has no other copy, some people are going to like you and some will not. But what you need to know is the way you have been drawn; you need to know that you are an art that has got no other match! You need to embrace your outlines, you need to celebrate your colours!~

~You got to let no one judge you, you can't stop them from judging you but what you can do is not get affected from their judgement! You gotta keep loving your drawing no matter if people find it enthralling or not!~

And that's all you've got to do! You got to love your own built and not care about what they think!

I want you to love yourself! I want you to forget all you've heard from others as to what kind of a person you are. I want you to look at yourself as if you are inch-perfect and you don't need no hate for yourself.

TINYYY!! Yes!! Youuuuu!! Don't need nobody to tell you that you got to love yourself.

You don't need nobody to make you feel that you are important, you got to know your worth and you got to get out of the dumps all by yourself.

~You got to make love to your 'me' before you make love to any other me!~

You were made in love and were meant to be! When I say this, I want to remind you that you got to keep that love vigorous. You don't have to let go of that feeling; and it should be first feeling that you shall be having for your own self. The feeling of LOVE

Do you even think of how opprobrium it must be to that power that is responsible for our creation?

Like we are simply letting that power down by counting flaws in its creation, the creation that was made with so much of love and sacrament.

~You are to be extolled and not criticized!~

The truth is that we all are flawless and we all are perfect!!

~And the ones which seem to be lacking that bright shine are the ones who have not believed in themselves, they haven't believed in themselves strong enough to make others believe in them.~

~Because till the time you don't get to know your worth, you can't tell the world that you are expensive! ~

You'll be regarded as exorbitant only when you'll showcase your spirit to them! And till the time your 'me' isn't confident about itself, it can't make a mark out there!

You don't have to let people do favours to you while

you sit back and watch, you got to get up and get your hustle on; to make them see your potential.

~You got to believe in your 'me' and you got to start balling for the things which really belong to you, they are lying out there, waiting for you to put your hands on them.~

So, from this very moment I want you to scream it out!

At the top of your lungs, scream out that, "I know me! I believe in me and I will love me!"

"I am no longer going to care about what they think of me, i'll do it for me! "

Louder!

And for real!

You got to do this! You need to love yourself and perk up yourself! You need to stand up and hit the shot as soon as the ball gets into your court!

You got to stop beating around the bush and start working on it instead.

You need to go ahead, believe in yourself and use your potential to the fullest and bang for your buck!!

You need get at it! From this very moment!

GET UP TINY! GO TO THE HUGE!!

[5]
"The power of me"

* * *

The strongest power that has ever existed is "the power of me".

Me has a power which is immensurable. Me is an individual which was sent down to do whatever it wanted.

Me has been exempted from all the barriers. Me does not have to think of people but "I".

Me has to be obsessed , self obsessed. Me has to know about "I" before it looks over anyone.

People would judge me! But real me remains unstirred.

Me has to be in no limits. It has no boundaries to be in.

If me feels like standing out in the crowd wearing her bikini, guess what? Me can!!

Me can wear as much short clothes as 'me' wants. Also Me can cover him/herself utterly in the hijab if 'me' wants.

Because; ~We have been sent here to do something "more than covering ourselves and judging others."~

What 'me' wears is of no concern, how or where 'me' lives shall be of no interest to others.

There are no distinctions for a good or bad 'me'.

If me feels like screaming "fuck you" at something, me can!

'Me' can stand up for his beliefs without thinking of what others will say about him! But 'me' has to educe that none of its action shall be hurting others. If me has to get selfish then me shall not forget that me has to learn to find way to its happiness alone, without taking any aid from the society!

Me has been credited with a mind and a soul. And that is all that 'me' has which is of its own.

Every other thing encountered by' me' is just a part of the process.

~The process is complicated yet trivial, the process is life!~

And to be the most prominent element of the process, 'me' will have to seize the best of the 'individual' qualities.

An immature 'me' will try to make its presence felt by being the volatile element of the process, but real me is going to be "distilled water"! It is going to be there in the reaction yet not going to bring any change! You are not going to find any chemical test for its presence, and it itself is going to serve the process in the most ameliorate way.

Real 'me' would be at peace! Not on outside! But in its mind!

Me can decide its fate! All 'me' needs to do is to

think about life in the most sackless way!

Me has to realise the need of discovering more about itself.

And the real power of me is its 'growth' !

So both of us are going to get in this fast lane together now!

Both of us together are going to encounter all THE ELEMENTS of the process now!

And yes I am going to take you ahead leaving you with all those questions all by yourself!

And don't tell me you have already forgot them!

[6]

"They are reactive! They are effective!"

* * *

They are them! Them is society!!

~Yes I don't drink, but I never thought a person who drinks to be vile !

Yes the smoke chokes me up but I never looked down to the smokers As if they are wicked?

Yes even if the girl next to me isn't dressed up the way I call it sassy , I don't call it trashy !

Yes we all are sole! Yes we gotta have a way to this life which is finite to us only!

Why do we have to judge others?

Why do we have to make it difficult for others?

Let's make it simple , let's just accept people for

what they are !

Let us make them feel snuggy bout pouring their heart out!

Let's make love and make most of it !!

LET'S DO THIS !~

And to counteract 'me' they are there!

The problem with me is that it is unable to know itself which lets the society to have a hands on access of 'me'.

Hey!

You?

TINY!!

Here you need to get into this now! As me!

You know? Why you have been feeling so weak about yourself? Because you have never been courageous enough to know who you are!

You have become nothing but just another bee in the trap!

And boommm!!.

You didn't even know you are trapped! You are letting them fasten their trap on you!

Their trap is wicked! Their trap is pessimistic! Their trap is unreal!

And why do you have to get into fraudulent when you deserve to be served with real authenticity.

The fact that you don't mind being a dumb shit is really intimidating!

You need to know that their filters are formidable and if you'll keep trying to pose the way they want you to then you are doing nothing but just letting them have the last laugh because to them nothing is going to be perfect and they'll make you lose yourself!

So, you need to stop making efforts to please them; the only person that you need to please is you yourself!

They will talk to you in a certain way today and they

will say something else tomorrow 'cause they have just not been able to figure out life. They are nothing but a wobbly stream of thoughts, always fluctuating.

~They are going to make nothing out of this life and they are going to make sure that you also don't.~

They are weak! And they want you to be weak too, they won't let you standout with your own views. At least not till you try to abide them.

To be strong you need to come out of the trap! To be real you need to follow your heart!

You are not going to be happy till the time you don't cut off the strands that are keeping you grounded, the strands that make you stay intact to them, the strands which are holding you to keep you in this malicious trap!

You will not be able to find out the peace till the time you don't learn to be all on your own.

~No matter how good they are! No matter how much they love you! The truth is you need to decide your fate on your own!~

Whatever they say comes from their preconditioning, and don't you think it's too main stream to follow what is being said without even getting to the roots of these sayings on your own?

They are a disease! It's severe, it's life taking! It may even kill you! Mentally, physically, it's just terrific.

And you my child gotta make sure that you don't get a catch of this disease, because once infected! There's no cure !

Mm hm. !

You can think about it...!

.

!

I know you don't want to be a part of this trap at all!

But then you also just can't help yourself.

lemme me help you right here!

You don't have to get out of the society, calm down! Stay there.

No! You can't even change them. Nah! They are rigid I told you.

Nae... you don't have to convince them that you don't agree with them but you a gem at heart.

And just stop!! you don't have to give up and walk on their steps like a loser.

Here it is what you have to do.!

It's the easiest and the most difficult way all at the same.

I call it easy 'cause I just made it and I know it simply happens in a free flow.

I call it difficult 'cause I know it's difficult for you, yes because you are trapped my child.

(no I am not under estimating you TINY, kudos to you if you have come out of this trap on your own! That's all I've wanted for you!)

Now getting back to the way!

The way is you! Everything is you!

All you have to do is to be you!

LET ME ELABORATE.....

The reason that you are hog-tied when it comes to cut off the strings is that you are weak, and you don't trust yourself enough to be able to standout.

You need to "BELIEVE" in yourself!

And that's the first and foremost thing you need in your life.

Until and unless you don't know who you are and what you want you are not going to be able to make it.

You need to know about your strengths and you got to believe in them.

You need to know things for yourself on your own.

ALL BY YOURSELF, ALL FOR YOURSELF! That is what you need.

You need to redefine a meaning for your life, a meaning that has no ascendancy from society.

Let's get this simple,

What you need to do is to know who you are.

And it's completely okay not to know the answer to this question! The problem would be if you get out of this life without getting this answer.

~And you have to know; you are not what people say about you but what you feel about yourself!~

Fat, slim, curvy, skinny is not a measure to your beauty. Black, white, brown colour of your body is not going to tell what kind of heart you have.

All covered, half naked, completely naked .. Your clothes are not going to tell what kind of thinking you have.

Rich or poor .. Your beliefs need to be richer.

'They' are always on a game! And you can play back!

Since, these are their measures, measures of the society!

And because they are going to measure your beauty with these filters, this makes you have an upper hand because they are going to make a wrong you out of you since they'll be using wrong measure to figure you out!

They are going to evaluate you for lesser points and once you know who you are you can show them how you are much more than what they thought of you!

~They don't know that the real you is what you are inside.

And that is the person they are never going to know of!~

It's not impossible but it's unyielding for them to look beyond these measures.

And you need to do this favour to yourself.

They cannot figure out the sneaky side of yours, you need to find out that on your own.

And make sure, you figure out that sneaky side without their assistance because if you get them engaged in this process then you'll be making it complicated on your own. Because that way, you'll end up being a part of their trap again!

TINY?

Just don't ignore your point of view when you find out that the people around you are not talking the same way.

That is you!

Every time you say something that people find weird, that's you!

The one that questions back when you are told something, that's you!

You know what?

Your inner self calls you.

Everyday! Every moment!

But you! You are lost.

You are trapped.

And this is where you need to start from, you need to let your inner voice come out.

Let that inner self take the charge of your life. Because it'll make you live a life that is created by you and not society.

If you need a reminder then do set this up as a reminder.

And also I have to tell you; you just don't have to read this!

Reading only, is not going to bring any change! You got to feel this way.

REMINDER.

'KNOW YOURSELF. BELIEVE IN YOURSELF AND YOUR POWERS.'

"COME OUT OF THEIR TRAP!"

SOCIETY'S PLOT.

It is annoying for me to accept the way I have been brought up by this society. We have been given a pre-planned planner and we are made to stick by it.

We have scheduled a perfect plan for all the age bars. A 3-4 year old child is expected to be sent to the play-way; the child is expected to complete his 10th grade by the age of 16 to 17 and then further expected to go to the high school and then college.

And then, 25 to 28 years of our age are seen as the perfect years of getting married. So we get tensed up about making our kids get married by that age!

All we are giving to our children is this set-up plan which we ourselves are not sure of.

We convince our children to choose the best subjects for them. We provide our children with the most expensive education but after their schooling we are worried about the kind of college that our children will get.

After college, getting a high paid job is the thing of concern. In this whole idea of leading to a successful life we are actually making our children lose their efficiency.

~The child who might have made a better vision out of this life is no longer able to think on his own. We are handicapping our youth. We are telling them so much that we don't letting them unearth this life on their own!

Our plan is not a proper getaway for success.~

What I feel is that, we do not have to be guardians of the future of our kids. We should leave them on their own.

Instead of telling them that how they should get

going in their lives we should tell them to make a thought of their own and then set a track to get on that point all by themselves.

~We are not letting our children to feel okay about being defeated! Such a world is restricted to a comfort zone and is not able to bear the raucous reality.~

~We are so scared of failures that we try to give a secure future to our kids! We ourselves are so weak that we can't nurture the minds of our kids with strength!~

~A mind with pre conceived notions cannot open up to new ideas. And we are providing those notions to our children and that is what is making them get scared of making a move which is out of their comfort zone.~

RISK. "risk" is the only factor that can lead us to the camouflaged riches of life.

And till the time we are `all talk and no doing' we cannot really bring the change which is actually required.

We need to take the risk of not teaching our kids anymore!

Everytime I tried to talk about this publically, the only response was, -" you will get to know that it's easier said than done! "you won't be able to stand by these beliefs once you'll have your own children!

And these are the people who are rigid and are not ready to be a part of the change!

It is sad to know that not only we are holding back ourselves from making moves of change but also we are trying to give a pullback to the people who want to bring a change.

The legacy that we have is that whatever has been set up by our great grand generation is the only right way to get through this life for us. And the young blood is considered not to be old and great enough to think of bringing any change to that.

I never really tried to give answers to that hot air. But what I know is that I am not going to give any of these prejudices to my children.

I would leave my children to get a meaning to this life on their own. Because I would be glad to hear another story from them.

When they will themselves decide what they want in their life and how they want to make that happen is going to be the only time when they'll accomplish great things in their lives.

TINY!

I want you to do this too! I want you to raise a generation without feeding their brains with your knowledge!

~Let us together raise a generation which is not guided by us! Let us see, how free minds will float in a stream of higher ideas!~

We got to put a sock on the mouths of people with a mind that is a tough nut to crack.

We need to stop being scared of not having all sorts of secured plans for our future and we should rather try to enjoy the things and the moments that are coming to us in this timeline.

To make our parachute fly we need to set it free from the attached strings!

Till the time we don't make a jump we cannot get our parachute opened. And we will not get to have that wonderful experience that would be for lifetime.

~Our initial hesitance is creating a distance between us and our dreamful experiences and because we are scared to take chances we are not making that jump.~

Trust me, try n jump! You are not going to fall , god is there to open that parachute for you and to make you land in another paradise. But what you need to do is to take risk and have faith in yourself and faith in that lord.

~We all will get to live this life till the time we are alive but the after hours would treat us based on the life we lived while we were alive.~

A congenial life will never give us a chance to experience the versatility of the life.

We are restricting ourselves to a particular section by not opening up to the freakish ideas which lay out there.

As I read about the humans of world, what makes me feel happy is that not everyone in our society is weak some of us have shown immense strength of smiling through the toughest of times without any sign of pain on their face.

Not all of us are weak, some of us are really daring and have been hands on to the risk and such people are the real 'winners' of life cause they have been able to find out their happiness in the li'l moments of the life and they admire the beauty of the universe.

These are the people, who have got to know that how a dark night leads to b'ful mornings.

Let us together take a moment to forget whatever we have learned from this society as of now!

Let's unlearn whatever we have been taught by the society!

~Let's discover ourselves and our lives on our own terms.

UNINFLUENCED, UNCHANGING, UNDEVIATED. ~

REMINDER

`let's have faith in ourselves and faith in the power of lord.'

Let's go ahead stronger, together.

10 things you don't have to tell them.

1. Who you are! **You just don't have to tell them who you really are**.
   Let them judge you for what you are not! Let them assume things.
   You have to know who you are from insides regardless of the outer picture that they have in their minds for you. You need to be aware of all your valleys and peaks and you need be aware of your seldomness. You got to stay low key, you need to know your value!
   It's not them who need to know you but you yourself, so you need to explore the soul that's inside you not for the sake of telling the society who you are but for the sake of bringing another selcouth being to the world.

2. What you can do! **You don't have to tell them what all you can do.**
   Society is going to under-estimate you! And that is the key that is the way you can turn yourself on!
   For every time you are belittled, you need to get your hustle game stronger and you gotta hit harder instead of giving explanations to your critics. You got to spend your time on making things happen instead!
   ~The only explanation your critics deserve is your success!~
   'Vindications' are nothing but a proof to the fact that you lack that faith in yourself! For if you are fully aware of your worth and when you know that you can do everything and anything you want, then you will never spend your time in the wasted explanations.

You need to know your strengths so well that you remain unaffected even when you are belittled by the society because you know you going to disprove them all . So,
"When they term you shoddy, you got to get your game stronger Broddy! "

.

(P.S. broddy is you tiny)

3. Why did you do it! **You don't have to explain them your actions !**
   Whatever you do, whatever you believe in, it's all an individual choice that you make for yourself.
   And you don't owe any explanations to anybody!
   Even when you see them dispraising you for your actions, you don't have to change your actions. You don't have to change a single action of yourself just to please the society!
   The only concern is, it should be of no harm to others! Else, you don't have to settle for anything less than what your heart wants.
   You got to do your thing! You got to do it your way! People are not always going to love you anyway! But you can love yourself in each and every way.
   And if you love yourself real enough, you got to do all it takes to make your move without really caring of the backlash you get from the society!

4. What you really meant! **You don't have to untangle their thoughts about the things you say!**
   It ain't your problem if they misinterpret what you say! You just got to be upfront, put your point of view across exactly the way it is! You don't have to change your words just to make them sound entrancing.

For if your words and your thoughts are being misjudged by somebody then it is just because they don't know you at all.
So for every time you are left in a place where you need to clear your part, tell yourself that you are stuck at the wrong place!
That is a place where you don't have to be, you don't belong there. And you! Can decide if you want to be a part of such situations or not. You can decide you are going to answer their questions or not.

5. Agree with them, even when you don't! **You don't have to nod a yes when your heart says no!**
For every time your heart says a 'No' make sure that your mouth speaks it out!
You need stop agreeing to things that you really don't agree with. You need to be able to stand out, stand out with a thought that is not mutual. Cause for everytime you say a 'yes' to a thing that you don't really agree to, you are losing one of your individual thought.
You are being ordinary and trust me you are not! You are more than that.
You need to feel comfortable about delineating your thoughts, you need to stick by your perception and not change it for any reason or anybody!
You need to feel good about the fact that your mind doesn't agree to what they say, that rebel in you shall grow! It shall not be masked by the supremacy of the society.

6. You are happy! **You don't have to tell them whether if you are happy or not!**
Your happiness is your treasure, it is your pleasure, and you need to embrace it all on your own!

Your happiness shall be your first priority and you shall not let anyone effect it.
~You shall spend every moment of your life in the vicinity of happiness, your life shall be a blooming paradise with the effervescence of happiness and it shall be watered with optimism everday!~
What you really need to know is that your happiness is not to explained.
You don't have to tell others that you are content with your life or not. You have to know this within and not let it out.
For if you are telling people that I am happy then it is nothing but your weaker psyche that's actually trying to convince itself that it's happy. And because it's not sure whether if it's happy, it tries to convince others to believe it when it itself lacks faith in its self belief.
~You don't talk happiness, you feel happiness!~
So make sure you are feeling more of it in your life and not just talking about it!

7. You are alone! **You don't have to tell them that you are alone and crave for their attention!**
'I am alone' says the weakest person ever!
No strong person has ever said that I am alone and felt bad about it!
For being alone has been a strength to every strong person, and if you were crying about your loneliness, I want you to get your back up right now!
I want you to tell yourself that it is you who needs to stand by you! And till the time you have your faith within you, you are not alone! Nobody is going to come up to be a companion of your soul and bring you out of your loneliness; you need your back to yourself and if you don't stay there for yourself then nobody else can

help you to curb that loneliness.
What you need is a single moment of realisation that 'you are the first person you need'.

8. To believe in you! **You don't have to tell them to believe in you!**
   You don't have to seek believence from society!
   If you believe in yourself then there's nothing in this world that can let you down!
   If you believe in yourself then there's nothing in this world that you can't achieve!
   And if you believe in yourself then there's nothing in this world that can make you change your plans!
   'self-belief' is the strongest emotion and once you have that emotion in you; you'll be stronger and you'd be ready to accept all the knock downs with a sport spirit. Believing in yourself will make you confident about the things you do and you'd not really care if people are in awe of you or not.

9. Why you are different! **You don't have to tell them why you are different!**
   You need to work hard, you need to lose your sleep if it takes that; stay focussed; go extra miles but what you don't have to do is to explain the society how you are different!
   Weak speaks more, stronger stays calm! If there's somebody who needs to say that you're different, it's the society!!
   You need to let them see your uniqueness and appreciate you for that!

10. To love you! **You don't have to tell them to love you!**
    Love is not to be asked for!

It is the most pure form of a power that has ever made its existence!
And this power is way too strong to be forced on someone; you just can't make somebody feel the ecstasy of love just by the outer romance. What it really takes is the romance of the souls; it takes the messing up of the strands of two souls so bad that they can't be untangled!
~Love is the most phenomenal process; it is the most spiritual association that exists between two souls!~
When two souls have a romance where they talk of their darkest sins; when two souls uncover their blinds and let each other in, when two souls can feel each other as one even when miles apart, when two souls don't have to speak to explain themselves, it's LOVE!
A reaction where both the elements tend to lose their part into each other; and in the second stage the elements show their properties in one another and eventually end up as a single element in the final stage! It is a reaction of love!
Love cannot be made so easily and once made it can't be eliminated easily!
So for if you're thinking that you can have love by asking for it, you are mistaken! Your love would come to you on its own!
And if you feel it's taking too long of a time, you need to stay there for it until it comes; you just don't have to give up!
Rushing into love is the biggest mistake that people are making these days, if it doesn't seems to be alright, it's not love! You have rushed into wrong love then!
If you don't feel those deep emotions which don't really talk but exist in the silence of the moments then you are in wrong love! If you don't feel the spirituality and that connection of equally tangled strands, you are in

wrong love!

And till the time you don't know on your own what your love would be about, you are going to end up in the wrong love!

~Just for the sake of being in love don't settle for a love that amounts lesser than the amount of love your soul actually needs!~

Because the counterpart to your soul does exist, and every time you try to rush, you end up with a wrong reaction!

This process needs utmost specificity and you need to make sure that you have that knowledge of unearthing the best and the real meaning of your love!

Don't rush into love, every love is love but not every love cannot amount the love that your soul really needs. So what you have to do is, not to fall weak! You have to believe in your love before you have it! And you got to stop accepting anything that comes across to feed your soul, you got to wait for your real counterpart so that you don't end up getting hurt again and again!

"If it doesn't feels alright, it's not alright!"

(TINY BOI!

for you to get things in your head, I've elaborated it all for you!

You just need to feel more as you follow!)

[7] Woman!

~I came across a lot of powers,

But one thing that was real distinct was WOMAN

No two of them were same yet they all were one.

ONE of a creation with no flaws, yet always trying to get better!

ONE power that was most determined to rise.

ONE power that couldn't be tamed.

ONE power you just can't get away with.

ONE power that's always giving away as much as it could.

ONE that just could not be described.

Here's a toast to all the woman who know what they are, and the ones who don't let go of any chance to cherish their beauty.

Here's to the one's spreading smiles, trashing away

damned negativity and spreading all the positivity.~

Being a girl, I would surely not let go of this moment without rendering my thoughts over the scenario that has been created by our society for a woman.

The world that we are living in; a woman is the highly judged and the most criticised element here!

Passing their two cents worth comments on a lady is the favourite thing for people to do.

I don't know what makes them have a charge of deciding the limits for a woman. What I can deduce out of their deeds is that they are scared of 'women' as well.

~ For they know how fierce she can be, they try to cage her up. Because once set free, she can set fire to all of them.

Her fire burns sinner and it gives warmth to the martyr on a cold winter evening.~

~She can be anything from a drop of water to an ocean with heavy tide. And that can be the only reason why they try to contain her as to when she'll be set free she will only grow.~

It is the insecurity of our society that forces them to have such judgements to bring 'women' down.

It's a loud-spoken truth that women have been triumphing over the entire terrene.

And they fear being ruled by women so much that they try to limit their growth!

The sad-story is that people in our society are still living in their old classics; they might be living in big mansions but their brains are still hut-sized, they still want their girl to stay covered.

They warn their daughters that people out there are not trustworthy. They are quick in disowning their daughters if they do something which "according to them" has ruined their public image.

No matter how modern our outlooks are we are still fighting with the plague. Plague of discrimination between a girl and a boy.

I feel so blessed that I have I have managed to make a mark in the society on my own so that I can bring out my voice today. But what makes my heart ponder in pain is the fact that a large portion of our society is still not giving their daughters the kind of love and support they need in their lives. And keeping this problem in my mind I am not going to waste my time in convincing the society; yet again! Because I know that will not be worth it.

I would rather try to tell this to my 'youngstars' that they don't have to convince the society anymore! All they have to do is convince themselves.

We all need to be a part of this to remove this plague from its roots. We need to change our mindsets instead of telling people to do so!

All you have to do is to be sure that what you are doing is not wrong and if you are sure that you are right then you don't have to give them any butt-ass-ducks!

TINY, no matter if you are a girl or boy. What matters here is that we need to sensitise our minds about issues like these. We need to give all the required attention to this because we are the ones who'll be raising the future generations.

We can take the lead and we can make a lead!

Lead to a world full of prosperity and equality.

What you have to do is to make sure that when you see a woman, you are not telling her about her limits. You need to get this in your head that there are no limits for anyone!

No matter if a girl goes out with every random guy every night! No matter if she speaks in a manner that holds no conformity.

It gives you no sovereignty of criticizing her.

You do you and let her do her!

Her clothes, her habits are no measure to her character!

And you are no one to characterise her!

~So is a man and so should be a woman!~

The world has got all sorts of flavour, flavours of human behaviour! And it's difficult to categorise a lot of people in same section and that may not be correct as well!

It's not only the society that is hindering in the path of the women but there are women doing it on their own as well!

And hence, keeping this in mind, I'd take a moment to mention those ladies who are trying to pull down other ladies.

~Women will grow only when they support each other, society is enough to decimate us. ~

~We got to stand up for each other. By each other's side, strong and tall! We need to be on the same team; give up on that creepy back-bitching shit.~

~Let us rather be the front queens! Slaying on the front rows, let's not do any back stuff, let us be all about front stuff!~

~To the ladies who are trying to seek fake attention in the name of feminism, you are being looked at! You need to change your game plan!~

~ And to the society that's tryna stop women by making chicken shit rules for us to stand by.

Real ladies are taking over! You better watch it!~

And here's to not just the men but also to the women who think there ought to be any limits for a 'woman'.

To all those people of this society who tend to drag women as low as their opinions. Who believe there are certain limits to the way they should be living.

To the ones who think she'd look better covered, it'd be better if slangs aren't a part of the way she speaks and to the ones who are like - that girl? The one who smokes? Yaaaaa I tell you youuu!!

Bros go get a life!

She ain't no material that can be put into jars or bars.

You need to see her ablaze. And if you are weak you need to burn for sure!

And also ladies, don't you let yourself be a part of things which really don't exist. Don't cooperate with their imaginary image of how a lady should behave. It's you who is supposed to give an individual meaning to WOMAN.

DON'T LET THEM DECIDE WHO YOU SHOULD BE.

Stay naked if u don't like clothes, drink all day if you feel like boozing, smoke smoke all day long, speak whatever language you want. !

But just BE YOURSELF!

M never settling for their distinctions and I know you also won't.

~She,
Should have been in a veil
But went out naked.

She,
Should have been speaking tenuously
But was strident on the mic.

She,
Should have been in the kitchen
But was on voyage.

She,

Should have been with a man
But was with the hardihood.

She,
Should have been what they wanted
But was herself.~
~Stop calling yaself a 'woman' for effsake!

Just coz you got them enlarged breasts and the vagina it ain't making you a woman!!

You need to see the beauty others have in them to be a "woman".

You need to lift others instead of pulling them down to be a "woman".

You need to cherish the beauty that lies behind all the darks of life to be a "woman".

You need end this 'bitch I am going to fuck your life' for a revenge to be a "woman"

You need to play slay game strong to be a "woman".

You need to gotta be real elf to be a "woman".

You can't lay back and judge them ballin' and be a woman!

You need to get up, do your thing and let them judge you instead, to be a "woman"~

[8]

My alter ego!

* * *

~Had his eyes open but could not see the truth,
Dumbchild, wasted half of its youth.
.
Lord called upon to raise a question on him,
He said could not see anything; lights were dim.

Lord lightened up the light,
He complained it was too bright.

Lord asked what did you make out of this life?
He said megabucks and the prettiest wife.

Lord asked what he knew of his soul,
He said, your question seems foul.

Lord declared! You lost,
The game that you played, where I was the host.~

And it could no longer hold itself!

She won't let me proceed any longer so I'd better let her have the charge to lead you forward.

Um hm,

This is the high time that I introduce you to my alter ego.

After all she is the one who has made me come across all these discoveries that I've made throughout this time.

And she won't let me ball alone ever. At least from now onwards.

Also, let me be honest she has always been the trump; the better part of me.

And yaaaaa!! She always had an upper hand in this game.

She's Li , better part of Sonali.

For the world I have always been Sonali, but to myself I'm Li.

Sonali is someone people know of on their n terms, Li is self made.

Li in me was discovered by Sonali on her long metro journeys!

I had to travel for as long as 6-7 hours a day to make way to college and back, which was extremely exhausting. This long journey was no longer exhausting when I confronted Li.

Li is no one but the rebel in me.

~ Li is someone who was never ready to accept the norms of society and was always curious to make a way to the casket of secrets of life.~

While going to bus then metro and then back to

bus, according to people I was wasting my time. But hardly did they know that all this time, I was unveiling the hidden truths of life.

That lonesome time was the best time; I could manage to think of all the aspects of life with Li in that time.

Sitting quiet and looking around with my reverie and wandering imagination and spinning my yarn about life was a form of meditation to me. And I used to do that for more than 6 hours a day.

And this meditation carved a way for me to my inner self. It helped me to know myself for my soul and not my body.

This sprouting alter ego was observed by me when I realised that I am not what they think of me, every time I used to hear something about me which was not really me, it made me wonder why can't they know me for who I am.

I may sound cray! But it is what it is!

We are two!

~We all are two; one that lies inside us and the one that is seen on the outsides!~

Now, Let us both (Sonali&Li) just get started and bring you back to the reality check that we were having on life, on society; how it is effecting us, and is not letting us stay the way we actually are.

Li too has a word to share on this!

Sonali as a child could never think any deep, I had never been any curious child.

Li ,my better half , came into existence; some two years back may be!

Or exactly after I was waken up from that one bad dream!

Ever since then Li has been guiding me to the lights.

Li made me think about this fact that how irrational distinctions our society has made.

And how we cannot go up the creak without paddle; and just how we feel taped out when it comes to lift ourselves up out of that trap. And I would have been a part of that trap too if it would not have been for Li.

Li helped me to explore this life; she helped me not to agree to whatever they said.

Starting from the way this society has given us a thought of how a person should get dressed; they have made us see our bodies in such a way that they cannot be left naked.

And I am not going to lie saying that I had been cool about seeing naked people, like ever!

But Li brought better visions to me.

It was Li who made me believe that there ought to be no particular way of dressing.

I love clothes! And I am nowhere in a mood of giving them up.

But tinies! I do no fault-finding! I don't care what the other person wears or not!

~And if no one out of us would have been judgemental about the person besides us,

It would have been all solved.~

~To evlove and to grow in this life you will have to stay open,

Open to changes and open to acceptance,

Acceptance of rare things!~

The fact that we are served with the preconditionings is the most annoying one.

These perconditiongs are the reason that most of us are not able to evolve and think of this life on our own terms.

~What does a child get from this society?

Li says- "A bucket full of lies".~

Lies about life, all these lies come from people who

are not able to know what life is, people who are not able to have a broad vision, and people who cannot believe that something other ordinary can also happen.

~People who are rigid about their thoughts of an ideal life, are serving us. ~

And to come out of the trap of misconceptions you need to make sure that you don't sit and get served by them.

~You got to get up and serve yourself, serve yourself with the craziest philosophies, even if they are really crazy and right in no way, you will at least know that how to come across the right ones.~

If whatever you will do is on your own terms, you will never relinquish, because blaming yourself won't be easy!

And that way, you'd be looking for changing things into better instead of sitting, doing nothing and complaining.

And for this moment I would like to stop blaming society for every single problem that we have in problem our lives,

~Because we are ourselves being the crux of the matter; the reason that we are thinking way too much about the fact what others think of us is bringing all the complications in the process of life.~

Li says- "Can we, for the eff sake, not think of what people have to say about us? Like c'mon you don't have to please anyone to make yourself happy, and if, even for a moment you are giving up on yourself to make something else stay in your life then, you have mistaken and my child you need to start your game over again!."

Who is the producer of the society? We!

Who's the director of society? We!

Li says-"What are we giving to the society is what we are going to get back!"

So make sure you give your best into this!

~If we would have told our children to just go and give a meaning to life on their own. We would have come across mind-blogging thoughts and unnumberable meanings of this life.~

But!

~Li says- "The problem with us is that we think we have known enough about this life and we want our children to know the life in a same way as ours. We are not willing to let them tell us what this life is about."

"But the truth is it doesn't take ages to know what life is about, but a moment.~

I do remember various happenings of my past which were okay to me as Sonali, but then Li came over and made me think about them over again.

Being grown up in an Indian family, like any other Indian girl, I too had never been exposed to the vulgarities of life.

Here in India, we try to keep our children "safe" at least according to our culture, it is safest option to keep our children away from any vulgarity that lies out there.

We try that no li'l kid gets under any bad influence and comes across no profanity.

And this reminds me of my reciprocation to this thing,

When I got into a new high school. I had a lot of alarming moments.

.

.

.

.

One day our English teacher made us play a game, where she gave names of different classmates to each of the student and students were expected to give a single word describing the person whose name was given to them.

The game continued and the so called cutest guy of our class got my name and the word that he addressed me with was "tall".

Now that was the weirdest way in which I was ever described.

Not because of the word I call it weird but because that person could not see anything in me accept my height; what I felt was that the answer should have been emotional and not materialistic.

And as Sonali I could not get any real closure to this affair and sadly at that time I hadn't met Li so I over-thought and tangled the strands of my mind and all I could conclude was that " I am not fascinating enough and that guy is too cute to notice anything in me.."

But on the other side I thought, maybe he likes me? Does he like the fact that I'm tall? Can someone love somebody for being tall? ". What would noticing someone's height mean that was all Sonali could think of.

But today when I have descried Li; I was forced to rethink of that moment, and again relate to this fact that how we are actually 'judging people instead of knowing them'.

We show no interest to know a person till the time that person doesn't please our sight.

~We are not able to look into people because we are way too busy in looking onto them.~

That is what needs to be changed, and that is what we have to do! We have to try to know people based on their hearts and not body. This is what we need to give our society, "a non judgemental thinking" .

Thinking of my high school reminds me recall my first day at my new school yet again.

One bizarre happening which really sticks close to

my heart!

On my first day in my new high school, all I got to hear of was the "vulgerest" terms that I could ever come across! starting from the assembly lines ending to the class-room benches, all I could hear was students calling each other names; bullying, making fun of each other. Abusing each other to the worst level and laughing back to the death; that is how students enjoyed there.

And when I was told about the meanings of those slangs I found nothing wrong or vulgar about them. Because to a medical student, they were just genitals!

Still, I went back home, thinking and trying to find out the bad meaning out of it.

Today as Li I could know that I need to be so happy about this thing, that unlike all other students who were in my circumambience, I didn't find anything to be hyped in those slangs, I find them as nothing but just the other terms, terms used to retrieve more of our emotions than other words don't express at times , maybe?

And this makes Li speak even more!

"When in this life are we going to let go of the pussies and the dicks and give importance to the walls and bricks?

Yes Li is talking about building walls; building a wall barricading the judgements and our preconditioning, with the bricks of love, acceptance, faith and believance .

Another moment that I can recall right now is not from far past but just a couple of years old. It was the time when we had one of our family gatherings; wherein my cousin brother's family made a visit to my place.

My cousin had an eight year old daughter.

Me and my sister were sitting beside each other, and our niece came over to us and my dad standing over there just popped a question to her -"Ekta! Which aunt do you like?

And she pointed her finger to my elder sister. That was okay to hear as answer because my elder sister jells up with kids more.

But then my dad asked her why not aunt sonali? And to this she replied -"she has marks on her face and she isn't even fair."

And that was disturbing for me to hear!

At that day I could say nothing about it, cause I myself had no answer to that situation for myself. Because the truth was that somewhere, deep down inside; I myself was affected with those scars and my brown body and I did feel like they were a curse to me."

But today, when I have evolved and when my better half Li is by my side. I have learned nothing but to love every single scar of mine.

Scars not just on my body, but the scars which life gives in secrecy are also cherished by me today.

My complexion can no more bring me down because my shine comes from within and what I have learned over time is ~you got to love yourself on your own and they will themselves be attracted to love you. Also you don't have to care about them to love you, a strong and positive personality never goes unnoticed.~

The point that Li really wants to raise over here is that we haven't let the children to be free from these preconditioning and that is what is making them judge the rest of the people on these materialistic measures, the measures which are being used by rest of the society.

It's never too late, and this is for real. Throughout your lifetime, you can always build steps to betterment.

We cannot change others, but we can change ourselves! 'We have all the required resources to change ourselves'. And the truth is that all we need to do in this life is for ourselves.

"The process of life is of an individual surrounded by other individuals and within this process we need to proceed alone and the other souls surrounding us need to proceed on their own. All these individual souls are the different elements of the reaction to complete the process of life, but the reason that the process is getting complicated is that we are mixing up the elements, which means that we are trying to build non-existent relations between all of these elements.

The mantra is simple, in order to let the process go smooth we need to stop relating us to others.

And we need to give our individual potential to be in the reaction and we don't have to end up as an element mixed with another element.

We need to make sure that we come out as an individual end product.

And now! Can we? For a moment? Start all over again like a li'l kid!

With no preconditioning, no knowledge.

Let's get back to the first empty paper of our notebooks and write the story again.

This time! Just for ourselves!

Our individual story, unaffected...

[9]
And to win this life game,

* * *

You got to learn not to blame....

Yes, you need to get ready to fall, get ready to accept things just the way they come to you.

You don't have to get disheartened if the things don't fall into places or if things don't happen the way you thought they were going to happen.

"It's easier said than done!" I think these kinds of statements are made by the people who are not really willing to do anything big in their lives.

Excuses! giving excuses is the best thing that weak people can do and they try to make themselves sound unalloyed.

When weak people are not able to achieve big things; they try to make excuses as to clear their part. They try to spin a yarn as to justify their actions and to explain why they could not make it happen.

And I have real examples to clear my part on this!

It was the last month, this year when I had to head for a "National conference for a safer and convenient taxi in India".

On the day 2 of the conference physically challenged people were called upon to share their stories about how they have to deal with traffic related complications in their lives.

I am an emotional person, and I do feel others pain way too deeply but my heart was over whelmed that day not because of their disability but their ability of not giving up on the life in spite of being deprived of the ability of hearing, watching, speaking or even walking.

They had a mediator with them. And it was so heart warming to see them share their stories. One of them was dumb and deaf but he was a photographer; his passion to be a photographer was not crippled by his handicapped reality! He displayed his work and left everybody in complete awe!

Now the thing that was to be learned is that;

~ Those who have a will to do something in their life are never handicapped!~

'The ones who want to prosper in this life are making moves instead of sitting and complaining'.

None of these children or even the grownups was ready to sit back, they had accepted their weakness and moulded them into their strengths. They did not blame god for their disability but thanked god for giving them the ability of prospering with their determination to rise.

The day when I saw "differently-abled" quoted over a couple of seats in a DTC bus I could not hold back my heart from going into a series of heart-warming emotions.

This made Li reciprocate that we are completely responsible for deciding how we want our lives to be,

~Whether if we want to stay disabled or we want to get differently-abled. It's completely in our hands.~-

Only a few succeed in this game called "life" because only a few of us are able to take the charge on their own hands. Only a few of us are ready to accept the failures and not giving up.

Only a few out of us are okay to walk the other way when there is breakdown on one bridge. Only a few of us are ready to wait! Wait for the things to fall into places, the way we have ever dreamt of.

Only a few of us know about the power of me and only a few of us have been able to encounter the almighty power that holds the charge of our creation.

And my boy !

TINY boy;

Only these "only a few" are able to get what they want in their lives. And these few are the ones who win in this life game.

Yes! You can make anything happen; I will always say that but when it comes to the power of universe which decides our destiny we are laid back at times. There will be times where you won't end up getting what you exactly wanted.

And the mantra to accept failures of life is whatever has to happen, will happen.

Sometimes things won't come in our way as we want them to. But those are the times when we don't have to give up and move ahead even more strongly.

Let me spiel off an episode to you right here.

It was the January of 2016 when I was walking up the staircase to reach my classroom in my college which was on the fourth floor. I had my friend by my side and we both were chatting the time away as usual, suddenly a guy bumped into us and alluded me to give him a minute.

It made us halt; I questioned him in gesticulation about what was the reason of the hinderence. He looked over my friend, expecting her to leave but I intimated her not to leave! He asked me for my name and I replied him without any dramatic exaggeration. He further asked me if I had a boyfriend and I replied a `No' and just turned around, to get back on my way!

I answered his questions because I thought he was another guy who was being ragged by someone in the name of truth&dare!

Me and my friend were real queens to ignore shit real fast! So we did that as usual and went back to our class.

It was exactly some ten days later; that guy had sent me request on Facebook, followed me on Instagram and Snapchat. And as usual this new guy wasn't noticed by me until I started receiving some long text messages from no one but him!

He sent me a picture of me sitting in the A block of our university and described a whole long story of his love and demons. But then again I was not ready to give any attention to any of his diegesis.

Time was flowing his love was growing. He asked my friend about all of my past and tried to know as much of me as he could from others because I never talked to him.

He managed to have all the information of my batch, course, block, my phone no. and even time-table.

Over time he told the world of his love. All his friends used to tell him about my whereabouts in university. He would manage to catch a sight of me every single day and if he didn't, then he managed to find out if I came to the university that day or not.

He tried to convince me in every possible way that

he loved me like nobody else would. He told me that how he doesn't listen to Hindi songs any longer as to match taste of my interest.

He said that he comes to college by car now!

My Instagram made him think I was alcoholic and a smoke addict; so he got down on that stuff. He tried to do all the things that were on his level and even above. He thought he had to be 'my type'.

He got a wall of his room, completely overlayed by my pictures!

It was everything what a girl could ask for; A guy who'd do anything for her.

And after ignoring him to the best level I could not hold on myself from replying him and telling that he was wasting his time.

I told him that 'you won't have to change for someone who's yours! I feel mortified by all your efforts but that's more of hurting to me because I can't help you!'

I tried to explain this to him that his countless efforts would go wasted if he makes them on me because I didn't value them.

I didn't feel anything for him. And a single effort from somebody I love is going to be enough. I tried to tell him that ~efficient efforts at a wrong place are wasted!~

I know, Just a sight of me is enough for him to be happy! A day when I reply to his weeks or months old messages is a day of celebration for him!

Boy, if you are TINY today; I want to drop this for you right here, I do believe in miracles like anything but this miracle that you are expecting is not going to happen. I don't need to be convinced by someone to be my life partner it's a spiritual connection that goes on its own! I would get those vibes that I know I am going to have as to when that soul mate would be around me!

Whatever you do is admired, but this is just another thing in your life that you need to let go of!

You don't have to love somebody who doesn't value your love. The one who's meant to be yours will send back the equal amount of warmth to your soul as you'll send towards it.

I once wanted to know how someone cannot love somebody who does so much for them but now time has told me that the other person is not going to feel something just because you are making efforts for them.

~ It's love that needs to be felt in the first place.~

So to all of you who are reading this...If you also are making full-butt efforts for someone and getting half-ass attention in return then you are giving your time into the wrong thing. It's never too late and you can start over now!~

You don't have to be bulky or to look pretty to win this game.

Your skin tone, your body weight, your language is not going to give you any extra credits in this game. We all are on the same grade-scale and we all have to start from same level in spite of the difference in our possessions we all are on same level.

And the only thing that is going to make the difference is;

- The level of **determination**; determination to achieve what we want in our lives.
- The level of **consistency**; consistency in the hard work that we put in to get what we want.
- The level of **believing**; believing ourselves, believing our potential.
- The level of being **unaffected**; unaffected of the judgements of the society, unaffected of the fact that what they will think of me.

- The level of **acceptance**; acceptance of failures, accepting the fact that I need to improve myself, acceptance of unexpected situations.
- And finally! The level of **faith**; faith! In that almighty! The almighty power that created us!

10 things you shall not be afraid of doing.

1. What your heart says!
   Don't ever be afraid of doing things that your heart says!
   No matter if the sound from your heart actually makes sense or not! You are supposed to follow it!
   For once and all, you are required to do things blindly without caring about what the result could be.
   You need to give up on being so secure and not opening up to risks!
   ~To encounter the magic in your life, you'll have to take risks and you can take risk only when you follow your heart with all faith.~
   It is your head that stops you from doing things that don't seem to be easy, your mind is the one that makes you rethink on the decisions that are made by your heart and it often makes you to give up on that idea!
   And if you'll follow your heart, you'll yourself be able to take risks and you'll also be ready to deal with the after effects because you'd know that it was your decision after all!
   You'll feel the strength that would come to you from within.
   ~TAKE RISKS TINY BOI!~

2. **The things that are out of your comfort zone!**
   Don't be afraid of doing things that aren't in your comfort zone!
   What you shall not be afraid of doing is, the things that you are not really used to!
   You shall be open to tests, testing your capability by exposing it to the things that it has never encountered before!
   'Because to find out something unseen, you need to get yourself into the situations that you aren't accustomed to.'
   ~ The only way you can get into the door of the mysteries is by getting out of the zone that you have always been in! ~
   And once you get out of your home zone, you'll be confronted to the most incredible experiences. You'll be able to be a part of the situations that you wouldn't have thought of!

3. **Letting go of things!**
   Don't be afraid of letting go of things.
   And all the string that you are holding on to, are credent enough to give you the feeling of security.
   We are afraid of letting go of these strings because we don't believe ourselves enough; we don't believe that we can lift ourselves without holding on to other strings.
   And till the time we don't detach ourselves from all the external strands and hold ourselves up from within, we can't stand by the difficulties that life has in its stock for us.
   We ourselves make it complicated by not forgetting the things which have happened to us in past, we think of them even when they are gone and it doesn't let us to make the better of the situation that we are in present.

~If you survived alive out of a valley and you can still breathe, it simply means that you are still required to make a living, and this time you need to do that by being the better version of yourself.~
"You need to let go of old things and head over to new things with a fresh and more bloomed mind."

4. **Taking risks for the things you want!**
   Don't be afraid of taking risks for the things you want!
   ~To have things in your life, you'll have to step forward even when you can't see what'll come ahead.~
   You need to walk on the path which will lead you to your ultimate goal without really thinking of the obstacles that you'll have to encounter on the go.
   You can never know what is going to happen next,
   but what you can tell yourself is that no matter what may come you are going to get there! You are going to follow the path to your goal.
   You need to risk all your securities and go ahead by leaving them! Because to go forward you'll have to leave the things you had back then.

5. **Don't be afraid of doing the things that society terms as wrong!**
   You just don't have to think of whatever you have been taught till the day! What you need to do is, analyse things from your own perception. You got to find out what's right for you and you just don't have to care about what society has to say.
   ~Don't call a thing wrong till the time it has proved to be wrong to you!~
   Test the situations on your own, get your hands on to them just don't disregard them without even trying

them out.
Take chances, you can never know, which wrong may turn out to be right.

6. **Don't be afraid of achieving your goal.**
   You shall not be afraid of chasing your dream/goal. That is something you've to go after!
   You need to be patient enough to wait for the things to be the way you want them to be but you shall not stop pouring in your efforts to make things happen your way.
   Your goal will require your efforts and dedication but if you fall weak and if you're not confident enough about your dedication, you'll be laid back by the setbacks that'll come on the go.
   ~And if you're not afraid of the setbacks and if you're ready to go after your goal no matter how many times you get knocked down then you are going to get that success in every single way.~

7. **Don't be afraid of doing things that will make you lose your loved ones.**

   Now if you are thinking that what you'll say will make you lose your loved ones, then you are taking it all in a wrong way.
   Because if you have to hide your feelings or if you have to polish your thoughts before putting them forward to your loved ones then you are stuck in the wrong relationships. For real bonds cannot be broken by your real thoughts.
   If you are holding yourself back from being real you then you need to stop doing that and you need to come out of the company that you are in.

You need not to be afraid of being real thinking that it can make you lose somebody, you just have to be who you really are and let only those people stay in your life which are ready to accept real you!

8. **Don't be afraid of doing things you'll be judged for!**
   You don't really have to be hesitant about being judged!
   ~Every rich thing is judged by the poor ones.~
   That doesn't mean that it's not worth it, it's just that they can't afford it.
   The judging game is not going to end in our society any time sooner and it's better that we accept ourselves on our own and just stop caring about whether the society is going to accept us or not.

9. **Don't be afraid of Letting your heart out!**
   The life that we are living is uncertain and unpredictable. You may never know which thought could be the last thought of your life and therefore you shall not let things stay just in your heart or mind and not let them come out.
   ~Make things happen before you lose all the chances of turning them into reality.~
   You need to get all your emotions and fantasies out in your real world and live in them. You need to have things in your life the way you want. Once you get things in your head make sure you put effort to make them come out to your outer world as well.

10. **Don't be afraid of living**!
    Now!!
    When you're given this life, you are expected to test it to its extremities; you don't have to be afraid of living a life which is free!

Free from fear!
~You shall not be having any fear in your life cause the fear insides us, stops us from experiencing most of the beautiful things in our lives.~
So if you want to come across the surprising aspects of life, then you need to let go all forms of fear and you shall be ready to face any kind of situation that life puts you in.
~You shall enjoy every second of this journey, a journey which is completely decided by us!
We can make it a happy story or a sad story! We can call it a complete or an incomplete story!
It's all in our hands. So make sure your story gets completed and has a happy ending!~

[10]
Rich and the poor

* * *

The complaint that most of us have from the life is for the possessions that we've got.

Rich might be looking for a larger share in riches and the poor, for sure is blaming the lord for not granting him enough of possessions.

But to this Li has got a reply on behalf of lord. Li says that--~lord was running out of possessions may be, so he could not grant all of us with equal materialistic possessions but he made sure that we all could get those possessions on our own, and for this he granted POTENTIAL to all his creation.~

Because lord believed in his creation, he believed that they will make use of that potential on their own to get themselves to all of the riches which were out there.

Lord gave them the most powerful weapon, a weapon that could think. The weapon was brain! It could be used to think of any of the wildest thing and then that potential could be used to make that wild thought come into reality.

But, it is sad for the Lord to realise that his creation is lost in the self-made delusions of life. Its creation is so lost that it is doing nothing but complaining about not being rich enough to have all the luxuries in life.

~The poor is not poor until he decides to give up on the thought of making something big out of this life and just beg for things. ~

You don't need to have money to be rich but what you need to be rich is happiness. If your happiness is avaricious and it lies in the consumerist possessions then maybe someday you'll have your happiness and others day you may not have that happiness.

But if your happiness lies in small things like blue skies, waterfalls, dogs, family, love and the silence; then for sure your happiness is never going to dissipate.

I too want to possess a Rolls Royce and hit the streets of Vegas and New York, spreading smiles across the world and having all the fun of life!

I am not saying that you need to give up possessions but what I am saying is;

~ don't mix your dreams with your meaning of life.~

The mistake that we make is,

We think of these possessions as to be the only meaning of life, we think that owning most of the wealth would mean best of the life.

No!!

Best of the life would be having love, peace and faith!

These are the best ingredients for a happy life.

We all are mistaking life and we all are giving all of our hard work for earning money but when do we get to live the life?

Why are we spending our lives in gathering these possessions for us and then for our children and then for our grand children?

We should give them everything they need, but then we should not give them the preaching of always trying to gather materials instead of emotions.

~We all gotta die,
Everything else is a lie.
So as I live this life,
Imma make happiness rife.
All yae pretty souls together,
In the name of lord, happy forever.~

One fine day me and Li were having conversation and the metro journey seemed to be endless that day.

And talking to Li has been my kind of escape. And that day Li and me were making out a chronicle of lord and tiny!

Wherein tiny was the dumb little kid like us and was always complaining.

And you is that TINY today!

And that day tiny complained that why am I not as rich as the other people of the society.

And to this lord replied-" I am tired of their longings for being rich in owning the lands and territories, would you mind being rich in love and peace?'

Which is to mean that; the real happiness is being measured in the form of possessions by us! We are not really looking for peace but money.

But have we ever thought of the fact that when we die; we leave all of this wealth here! But the peace and serenity of our soul is what goes with us!

~So, instead of collecting possessions, let us collect moments.~

Another thing tiny asks is- "why did you give all your blessings to him and not me?"

Lord replies- "I gave the same blessings to you but you were too busy to realise".

We all have been equally blessed but only a few out of us are free enough to notice those blessings rest of us are just lost in the drama of life;

most of us are busy crying for things we don't have instead of being happy about the things that we possess!

Here, I want you to pen down 10 of your blessings, let's see how long does it take for you to think of just 10 of your blessings!

TINY, I want you to look beyond your perceptions now!

I want you to celebrate everything that you own!

I want you to start NOW! Right now!

The thing Li in me has discovered is that we all are going to leave this dream park and we may or may not go to the same places as to when we'll die.

~ But in the present moment we have got to share this lifetime, and what we can do for each other is spread love and smiles.~

And world cannot be richer than that, if there would be smile on each and every face in this universe then there would be no more longings for riches.

Cause a person who'll be happy in its skin would be making better out of this life instead of complaining!

~ A world full of love and smiles means a world that has accepted all the flaws and is ready to turn them into beauty.~-

It means a world that is no more scared of dying with little possession, a world that is always down to the power that owns it.

Such a world would always be heading way up! Because of such a world people would not be cursing the Lord for giving them less or more treasures.

~And in such a world people will themselves find ways of unrolling to the casket of treasure.~

"And such a world will have all rich no poor."

[11]
It can take you to the moon and then bring you back!

❄ ❄ ❄

It's a THOUGHT!

"Our thinking is our potential".

~If you can think properly, then you are filthy rich.~

You can call yourself poor or disabled only if you lack the power of thinking. And with god's grace no one out of us lacks this potential.

And what I am going to say next is the baffling truth of this life.

~Your life is nothing but a thought, it is just a thought we are living in,

And your thought is going to decide what kind of life you live,

Good thought means good life and a bad thought will get you nothing but a shoddy life.~

What you become in your mind is what you can be

in your life. Trust me tiny, it is as simple as that.

~This life can be decoded, and the weapon can be our mind.~

~Our mind is the most sumptuous ornament that we own! It is the way to all the treasures. In fact it is the only way to the treasures.~

Our mind is incalculable, it has the competence of seizing limitless and the most bizarre ideas.

It is our mind that can let us do wonders! Any desire or any emotion is an outcome of our thoughts, and it is our mind that gives us strength of working on the freakish thoughts of our mind. It makes us believe that it can happen.

And fortunately, we can beget our thought. They are all real .

~ We just need to bring the world of our mind to the world of verity.~

"The kind of thoughts we have is going to decide the kind of life we live."

Every single thought of ours is deciding our fate. Not many of us are really trying to figure out the reality of this life that we are living and that is the reason why we are not able to find out the measure of the power that we have within us.

~Li in me believes that this life happens as our thoughts happen.~

Every time I thought that something bad is going to happen it did happen to me. And every time I had been sure of my intuitions they always happened for real.

I believe that what my mind conceives is what happens to me in my life.

I have been able to control my thoughts and so am I able to sway most of the happenings of my life. It is my strong belief in my power of thoughts that makes me believe that I can control the things from happening.

What I can make out of this whole thing in regards to life is that we can fantasise our own mantra to decide the steps of proceedings in our life.

~Life is similar for all the individuals but the disparity lies in the way of fantasising.~

The way in which I may fantasise my life may not be same as yours. But the thing that is important is that the way should be of your own. Undecepted and unaffected from the views of others.

We can think of the weirdest possibilities of life and then mandate them as the yardstick of our life.

~The reason behind the success of discovering rarest things in the universe is the versatility of our mind. A curious mind would bring newest discoveries.~

Life is unlimited it holds no space, it is endless. It is as limitless as our thoughts. It can begin from a thing as tiny as a grain of sand to as big as the whole universe.

Before anything happens you need to set your thoughts in the lane of the thing you want to have; In my mind I have always seen a strong-ass go-getter with the purest heart, open to everything. And I have been able to be that, I have been able to live a life like that.

You need to leave no space for negativity. If there is any room for doubt in your mind then there are going to be laybacks in your life.

So to ensure that you make a way up, make sure that you don't have any negative vibes in your mind.

We as human beings are falling short in giving the best of our potential in this life.

I see the youth around me, what makes me feel bad is the kind of thoughts they have!

The thing that makes me feel bad is that giving up is the only thing they are good at.

~ They are always hands down on blaming their life. They are full of wrong assumptions of how life is making fun of them, when actually they themselves are making fun of life.~

I have always accepted people the way they are, being a sober person I have never been into smoking or drinking but the company that i've had since my school days has been of the chain smokers or the so called "stay high-people". And I have never had any will of getting high like them nor did I've had a wish of stopping them from doing the things they do.

But today, the thing that's kind of hurting me is that they no longer want to stay sober and feel the life. It would not have been hurting if they would have been able of having equal interest in the life in spite of being high.

But the problem now, is that all they feel is that the high time is the best time and in that way they are actually out casting the beauty of life.

I certainly cannot convince them to try n figure out how b'ful is this space that we are in, so I am going to let life happen to them.

'Cause self learned lessons are the only lessons that we need to have in this life'.

But if were reading this in your low time and I've hit your heart in any way TINY! then may be I've done my bit.

'We are weak'. We no longer hold the capacity of being hurt, we find it easier to give up on our lives.

And that is the worst thing that we are possibly doing . We were given this life for free, (maybe)! But we need to pay a good sum in return while we are living.

I don't really know where it ends. Obviously death is the end! But in terms of the stage which is decided by the lord to end our living session! That is what I am not aware of. When does this session begins and when does it ends is surreptitious.

~Life holds a lot of mystery in its coffer. And that is what makes it interesting, we can stack up the rows one by one and it would lead us to a place that we could not even imagine! Life is a process which is the most enticing one, and it is full of surprises!~

"Kids these days!"

Is the one sentence that no one of us possibly likes to hear any longer. It's a sure turn-off for us!

But being one of the kids I still have to make a remark on this!

We kids, no longer have patience to tolerate any downhill in our lives.

A single breakup, and we feel like we lost our lives!

We are ready to commit suicides and give up on our lives so easily!

We no longer have the strength of being a lone fighter; we feel so down alone that we are not able to get ourselves up!

~A failure in our path becomes a closure when we decide to settle down after it hits us!~

We can fight back! You can fight back!

TINY! You don't need nobody to tell you this time and again!

No I'm not saying that your problem is not a problem but what I am saying is out of 100 you have 10 problems and 90 blessings!

So now tell me? Did you make out any time to feel good about those blessings?

Were they given as much of attention as you gave to your problems?

That is what the problem is!

~We all are facing problems but only few of us are letting go of those bad situations and moving our thoughts to the blessings that we have. ~

Let me share a small message that I have for you!

May be it will be a booster for you as well if you are on your downtime!

Hey tiny?

This is for you!

You need to know you don't need nobody to know you!

You just need yourself to hold you up at your lows and higher at your highs!

You don't have to be heartbroken at pitty stuff that happens in life, hold on to the beautiful moments!

You don't have to think of things that make you feel low!

You just learn to let go! LET GO the pain.

You need to autosuggest your brain to be happy.

You need to look for nothing but your happiness.

And before looking for that in others!! You need to find that within yourself!

Don't let moments bring you down! Coz there could be no better life than the life we living. Buck up my child !!!

It's all so pretty and sappy out here!

Let's just take this moment to be even happier about what we are instead of crying over what we can't be!

DON'T JUST READ! FEEL IT!!

(Don't forget to mix your emotions in this!) You are pretty, you are the best you!

I've had a friend in school time who loved a girl, but that girl never ever talked to him. He was a crazy one-sided lover! He'd do anything to have her attention but she did not care about him at all.

She had always made it clear she wasn't inquisitive about him at all.

He would make cuts with blade on his forearm while sitting in the classroom just to get her attention! But it never worked.

And there was one other girl in our class who loved that guy (it was a triangle for real!) so she would also make cuts on her arms and legs. It was like they were playing some stupid game!

And this was a situation where I really did nothing because I myself could not think of a solution to it!

But my boy is now completely over that girl whom he loved and is all grown up out of that childhood love.

And he was able to love another girl all over again!

And this time, after a year of relationship they had to split due to family reasons! And he was, crushed yet again!

This time, he didn't give up on his life but he gave up on love! He's no longer into studies all he is into is being high.

It was his solution to the problem!

Another girl from my high school who was a cute li'l girl as short as 5'.

She had lost her mother in a very young age. She along with her siblings was raised by her dad.

Her dad being a business man could not manage to give much of attention to his children, and she being the younger kid was drawn off, she could not find a right way for herself and since eighth grade she got engaged with a group of chain smokers. They used to do all kinds of doping, they did petrol sniffing to milk sniffing.

She'd never come to school without a weed.

And this was causing her problems, she did not have her menstrual cycle and later she even had stones in her kidney.

It was exactly like giving up your own life cause

someone you loved has left you.

But now, when life happened to her, she managed to get out of that bad verse and live a life out of misery. When she got to know this life was worth to be felt and lived, she decided to join a rehab to get rid of her sniffing habits. ~A girl that could not spare a moment without being high was now able to live a life on real speed.~ She just could not give up on that habit till the time she auto suggested her brain that she to do it for herself!

~And a strong desire can be defeated by nothing!~

What Li has to say is that people get high as to escape from life. They want to have an easy escape from all of their problems.

'A youth that is so weak, a youth that cannot face the downfalls, for sure cannot lead to a better future'.

How can we even give up on a rebel that would get us out of the dreamland to an unseen world in the end.

~How can we even afford losing curiosity to know what will be served to us in the next moment.~

I would not forget to make a mention of another pure soul that I know!

My college mate, he has got the purest heart like any other pretty soul I know.

He usually decides to stay low! And is always hurting.

And the reason for his pain is also the "weird love".

No, love is my favourite emotion but I'm calling' it weird cause in some cases people have made it turn weird.

That boy! Likes a girl and that girl again likes another guy! And this is their short sad story.

What hurts me is that people love others before loving themselves and it hurts me cause I've been through this once and I try to give all the cure to such wounds cause I know how they hurt.

I know tiny, how condolence of people does not make any difference to us till the time they are from the person we want.

I have been a part of such 'weird love' situation. And what I am trying at every moment of my life is to tell people that their happiness comes from where they want it to.

~ If you will decide that eating chocolates will be the only way to make you happy then nothing else in this world is going to make you happy.

Happiness can be decided, we can decide what kind of things can affect us. And this makes me say that we should not let our happiness depend on anyone else but ourselves.~

(Here I have another booster for you!)

Hey so/un!

I had to tell you about you before you think of anyone else!

And you tiny boi ; belong to that chunk of pure souls that I have come across in this lifetime!

And I had to tell you this because most of these pure people could not look at what they have inside!

And they blame thyself, for not being good enough for others!

Without even realising that they are the best of them!

And my boi! Real things are going to stay by and rest all will leave coz they are just lessons!

I just want you to be selfish for once like, c'mon! You came here alone now all of a sudden you need any nig to be by your side?

.

Uh! No man!! People like you should know their beauty and worth

.

You need to get everything for yourself before you think of anyone else!

Now don't tell me that having someone in your life is what's going to make you happy!

You better get your shit straight that no other person but 'you' is the one who is going to decide where your happiness will come from!

.

If you gonna stay this stupid then no one trust me not even me! Or any no one is going to be there!

.

Listen?

It's your life game wherein you 've

All the fair chances to set the table as you want!

I just want you to be at something where you need to be!

We'd be leaving the paradise soon!

We'd all be going!

But just in case if it's okay for you to go off with random incomplete stuff !

There you go!

Keep goin! .

Ps- But-you are a gem! How bow shining?

It's you that I'm talking to right now! It's you who's supposed to shine right now!

You are not just a reader to me, you are just another person that I'm trying to help! Because what I have discovered in my life is flabbergasting to me! And I want to surprise as many souls as I possibly can!

Why are we making our minds too prone to breakage? We are making are making our minds!

~They are not open to acceptance and that is the reason when something unlooked for happens we feel wretched. ~

We are just not able to tolerate situations which are out of the blues for us. We are constantly creating thoughts, the thoughts which are more of fairly-tale kind and less of realism. We are looking for a dreamy world but we are not ready to face the d'ownfalls which will lead us to the dream land.

Unlike the kids who decide to give up so easily! I know another girl who's in my batch in college.

She lost her mother at a young age and her father left her alone to her grandparents when she was not even 10 years old. Her father left for Florida and never really made a comeback!

That li'l girl decided to be the support system to herself as her grandparents were old and she knew, she'll have to keep herself together on her own.

The thing of joy was that she didn't blame life for the situation she was put in. She decided to back herself up. And not to fall weak, ever! She was strong at her very young!

As her grandparents grew older, they could no longer take care of her and their aunt who was actually their neighbour with whom they had family like relations took charge of her. That lady already had two daughters and was not at all hesitant to give her love to the third one now.

Since that girl did not give up on life and accepted the downfalls with a smile she was sent to a family where all her wishes were made to come true. She was given immense love by that family. I do see that girl in my class everyday and she's the chirpiest girl of our class. She is always there to raise her voice for any cause.

She is amazing in debates and speeches. She's a bright lady, she didn't let anything take away her beauty!

Her smile with those dimples is strong and vivid.

And as I think of her right now I feel so good to be able to know those few people who did not give up on life even at their worst.

We are thinking but are thoughts are not of the right kind.

And just a thought is not going to work for us.

The thoughts we have should be worth it. They should be factual and actual.

The thought should be of becoming rich and not of others getting poor.

The thought should be of having fame, fame for good deeds.

The thought should be of having happiness, without hurting others. The thought should be of having inner peace, without causing troubles for the outer world.

We need to know what kind of thought we should have to make the result come out in our favour. When I say 'your life is going to be exactly the way you think' then with thought I mean the right thoughts!

You cannot think in the wrong way and then expect things to happen in the right way.

OUR LIFE IS ALL ABOUT OUR THOUGHTS!

Yesterday, I saw a lady standing beside a priest!

That man was assuring her that everything is going to get better in her life and she had a sense of relief when she knew that priest was going to cure all her pains.

And everything would be fine with her.

And most of us are doing this!! We are going to other people to tell us that everything is going to be alright.

Because we are not able to convince our souls on our own.

It is our belief that says that other people can cure our pains!

It is not that anybody else is helping us but it is a sinewy faith that we have in the fact that other people can help us!

The people who believe in themselves are the priest and they are assuring the weak people that they are going to help them in getting rid of their problems!

And because we trust them enough, they are able to help us!

If we had enough trust in ourselves and in our powers, we could have been our own priest!

10 Things your mind can do!

1. Your mind can help you to grow!
   Your mind can completely be your growth medicine, it can lift you up from the land and take you to the skies. The kind of material that you have stocked in your mind is going to build the mansion of your life!
   Your level of ideas is the foremost thing that decides whether you'll rise or fall in your life. Thus, to have that growth in your life you need to have a growing mindset.
   Your mindset shall be strong and stable, it shall not be moved by the storms that come up in the way of life.
   Your mindset shall be of rising, rising not by letting other down but by lifting them up as well.

2. Your mind attracts the situations that you become a part of.
   For as long as you'll say, that you feel like something wrong is going to happen, it'll happen in the wrong way!
   And if you have a positive approach to an upcoming situation it is not going to turn out to be a negative one.

And in that case, even if the thing doesn't happen your way, you accept it optimistically and you try to give better shot to it again; because that's what an optimistic person does.
~The rule is simple, a negative mind will always get caught up in the negative situations where as an optimistic mind will make out a positive way out of the same situation. ~
And that brings all the difference.
We look over the situations with a negative mindset and then we cry that nothing good happens to us but the truth is that we are not able to see the good that's happening to us.

3. It helps you to create a world within before it gets created in reality.
   What we call reality is the world that lies on the outsides.
   Our mind, allows us to dream of a world before it comes into existence. Our mind allows us to think of the things that haven't happened yet and thus, it is the most efficient worker, it makes us dream of a thing and then helps us to walk our way to that goal so that we can make that happen in our real life.
   And we can do big things in our lives only when our mind has thought of them before!
   So make sure, whatever you are thinking is good, because ~the powers in your life work on the plot that is set up by your mind.~

4. It can make you believe in wonders.
   And because your mind has no limits it can make you envisage the things that aren't a part of the normal world. It can make you think of the things which are

extraordinary.
If you chose to make your mind believe in these super things then you can actually make them a part of your real life.
~it's only you who can decide what your mind can contain and where it can be contained.~

5. It can build as well as spoil you.
   You need to stay humble in your mind, for if your mind becomes a victim of pride, it can spoil things. You need to be right kind of obsessed in your mind.
   You have to be sure that you don't become a victim of your own thoughts! Because sometimes, we get caught up in such thoughts which are not really veracious. And these are the thoughts which prove to be precarious for us.

6. It can contain everything!
   Your mind has limitless ample space that can be filled up with any and every thing!
   Your mind can contain things that are not only visible but even the things that aren't existent! It can be real dreamy and it can think of things which aren't even heard of! And that is what the best part is!
   We all can fantasise our own world, wherein we can decide everything on our own!

7. It is a gateway to the unseen space!
   Gateway, that is what our mind is, it can take us to any place at a particular instant of time.
   It takes us to whole another space, and it lets us live in that moment.
   We can get into that space and know of things that we aren't used to.

~ Every experience that we have in our lives is nothing but the experience that our mind had!~

8. It can bring all the happiness and peace.
   ~We read a lot of stuff, we tell our minds about it, but we don't really feed our brains in a way that can change our thought process!~
   We just go across the motivational stuff, we don't really stand by it and that is where all the difference lies. Till the time we don't accept all these sayings by our heart and make them a part of our behaviour, we'll not get any change.
   Also, to have that peace in our lives, we don't have to look for it on the outsides; we have to create it within our spirits. And for that, we need to free our brain from all the contemplations. We need to have thoughts which are pure and not disturbed. If you reach that level of contentment in your mind then you can have that peace within your soul, it's all chained.

9. It is the key to life!
   And when you have come up this much, let me tell you the secret!
   ~The secret key to your life is your mind!~ and you have been given this key since the day one of your existence what you need to learn is the art of using it!
   You need to know which the locks are where this key is going to fit in! You gotta use this key wisely. Once you'll know how it works, you'll be able to unlock most of the situations of your life.
   And TINY!
   I'll help you; I'll tell you how this key works.
   You need to go a li'l more ahead now!

10. "Your mind can work the magic!"
    It can make you believe in the craziest things and can also make you walk your way to those things in reality! It can give you the strength in believing the things that nobody else has talked about.
    You can work over your mind unabridgely, you can shape it in a way that makes you see every situation from its own perspective.
    What you can do with your mind is unpredictable!
    So, when you can create so much of magic in your mind and then in your life; what is it that you are waiting for? Y'all need to start working on your magic! Make sure you do it; don't end up as a mere audience because you are meant to be a performer, achiever and a lot more than that!
    Buck up!! TINY boy!

[12]
Ways to your goal!

* * *

Your goal is a thought that is away from you!

It's a desire that tempts you to make your way towards your goal.

Your desire, strengthens you to walk towards your goal passionately!

A strong desire has to be mixed with hard work and consistency! Just a desire cannot lead you to your goal!

To get closer to your goal, you need to work hard and you are required to make the best use of your potential!

~You are required to push yourself up! Up and above from the bottom line that you always settled at!~

You need to cross that line and this time; you need to exempt yourself from your limits!

If you thought that walking an hour long is the maximum you can do!

No, it's not! You just don't have to settle; you can go

another mile away. You can walk for another one hour! You can always do more than what you think is your last!

What you think is your last is the point from where you need to push yourself! That push is the one thing that's called for to familiarize you with the extent of your potential.

Let me make it easier!

The ways to a goal are :

-A strong **Desire** of reaching your goal.

If you want to be a model; you need that burning desire within you!

A desire that should be fierce and a desire that can calm down only when you get it!

To be that model that you want! You need to keep an exuberant desire of being one! No matter what may come; your desire should not go away!

Failures, heartbreaks, society; they all are the predators of your goal, they may even take your dream away!

``But if you got a dream, you need to protect it on your own".

And a strong desire will fuel you up to chase your goal and it won't let you be a prey to these predators!

-A quality **hard work** that amounts your goal.

You should be ready to give everything that is required for you to achieve your dream goal!

Your relentless efforts are required to make the things happen your way!

If you want that huge built!

You can't get it as you sit in front of computer screens, you'll have to get up!

You'll have to hit the gym! Hard and harder!! As hard as that built requires!

You need to work for it!

-**Consistenc**y; your walk towards your goal should

be consistent. The only stop should be your goal!

If you want to be a writer! You need to write!

Every day, every moment!

You got to write; on the paper, on your computers and in your mind!

You just don't have to stop!

-your **potential**; you don't know how much of potential lies within you and that is the advantage! Every time you encounter a valley, decide to lift yourself up! And your bounce back would show how much potential you had!

And you'd always be surprised to see different levels of your potential as you'll come out of different valleys.

~You won't know that you can walk with one leg; till the time one of your legs is broken down!

You won't know that you can still find a way to see the world even when you go blind; you won't know that till you lose your sight!~

~So, every time you'll face a valley, you are going to encounter a new sort of potential that you already possessed but you were not aware of it!~

-

.

.

We all say we have a goal! But how many of us are actually working for it? Or how many of us do even really know what a goal is?

How many of us are really ready to give everything it takes to meet the value of our goal?

Because if you belong to the chunk of those few people who know about their goal and are ready to work their ass out for it, then only you are applicable candidate to walk on the path of 'achieving a goal'.

For if you don't know what your goal is, you don't have to worry! Your goal can be as little as going to the water park on the weekend or it can be as big as climbing the mountain.

You can have small targets and join them as one goal. 'Achieving your goal means making your thought come into reality by putting your hard work and consistency together.'

We all can have an individual goal in our lives. And to reach our goal we need to keep walking towards it. We need to walk towards it with complete faith. We shall not get spooked by the failures! We might not achieve it in the first go, but eventually we will make a hold of it!

Your goal doesn't have to be the richest or the most famous person but it should be of having even the tiniest things that give happiness to your heart.

And if your goal is big, and you don't know how to make a way up that hill then you don't have to worry my child because no one actually knew a way other than putting their hard work and everything that it takes to reach their dreamy-success level.

You need to start from a zero level and go step by step; you need to set a target stair-case that will lead you to the goal floor. And this is how the game goes!

"If you got a goal, you need to protect it." Protect it from being crushed, crushed by the fear of losing. Meeting your dream is going to be the most difficult yet the most enticing journey at the same.

~The only difficulty that you will be facing would come from the times when you'd see things falling out and that is the only time when you will be tested. Tested for your hunger; hunger of being served with that dream. And trust me, the person who'd be hungry to death will be the only person to be served. ~

There is nothing in this universe that you can't have. You need to work for it by the sweat of your brow. You need to settle only when you crack the whip.

We've all got the same life but the difference lies in our level of struggle, struggle of feeding us with the right food to calm down our hunger.

~The poor remains poor if he decides to cry over his poverty! And the poor becomes an iconic figure in the world of sports, movies or any fame world if he decides to come out of the clutches of poverty. A poor who decides to cut down its roof and plans its growth on a new ground, has always made a new way through!~

~You need courage, enough of courage to step out of your snuggy shelters into the scorching heat of the sun. You need to get your shit together and just work for it every single day.

You need to shed blood on the carpet if it takes that!~

~Just a pure hunger to make your dream come true is going to be enough for you to get there. And if you not hungry my boy ! You getting no food!

And if you're really hungry but don't got no bucks to have that fancy food, yet again you can't have it if you don't pay for its value.~

10 reasons why you should do something in your life!

1. Because you are given potential!
~You've got no reason for doing nothing and you've got all the possible reasons of doing everything in your life.~
And when you are given potential, it is a clear proof that you're expected to make use of it!
You just can't let go of your potential in waste.
Your potential is mighty enough to get you everything you want in your life! And what you need to do is make the best use of it.
If you were not required to create anything marvellous or to do anything stupendous, you would not have been given this ability in the first place! And now, because we own it, it's loud and clear that we are supposed to make use of it and make achievements in our lives.

2. Because you are a creator!
~You have been provided with the immense ability of 'creating'. Not just a new species, you can add more of new artefacts to the world!
You can create, and then you can add that creation in the rat race that's going on out there!~
And when you can be a creator, you gotta create; as to give your share in this game!
You don't have to create big things to add up on the board.
You can create a thought, a belief and give it to the society! You can be, just yourself and give a different mortal to the society!
You can create love and spread it out in the world. You

can create a shed and provide shelter to the lost ones. You can create a feeling of peace and share with the people in your circumambience.
~You can create things as small as ants and just give them away in this zoo! Even your small ants are going to make a count. But you gotta make sure that you are making that contribution because no matter how useless it may seem to you, but your contribution has a place of it's in the equation of the universe.~

3. Because your existence shall not be a waste!
When you are given so much, you are called for making a mark!
The universe is always looking for the contributions that are made by all of us. And it's requisite that we make that grant.
When 'you' was created, you was expected to maintain its integrity and you shall make sure that it does stick to its oneness and give the world best out of its existence.
Your existence demands beneficence, it requires the benefit of not just you but the universe as well. And the universe will itself be benefited if you make the best of your potential to create the best of an article and give a worth to your existence.
~Your part is of an individual, and it can't be given to the universe by any other person. You gotta make your mark all by yourself and you gotta do that because you are a specific block in this game of universe which can't be moved by nobody else. So you are required to make that happen all on your own!~
You wouldn't have ever known this?
Is it so, TINY?
If this was hidden from you; I'm telling you right here that that creator, creation and the powerful block in

this life game is you!!!
You haven't even realised how significant your individuality is!

4. Because you need to give a meaning to your life!
You have to do something in your life because if you don't, your life is going to be meaningless.
And to make it countable you need to get up and start moving the blocks in this game! You need to be an active participant in the strong game that is being played out there by all the powers, altogether!
~The meaning of your life is important because we don't know if we really have to explain our life to anybody else once it gets over and if we have to! Then you can't start a topic with really knowing nothing about it! So to make sure that you can tell people anything about you or to make sure that the world is fully aware of you! You need to give a meaning to your life first!~
You need to give a meaning that is all by you and doesn't account for anybody else and you need to stand by it, throughout your life.

5. Because 'one shall swim when into the river'!
If you would not have been given this life there would have been no debate over the fact that you should be making moves and contributions in this space.
~But when you are brought into this river, river of emotions, creations, motions! You are now supposed to move your hands and feet to swim across, to stay alive!~
And to keep swimming is to keep doing things in your life!

6. Because' you' can be the history!

Say you not!!
TINY BOI!!
You want you to be all gone? No! You don't! You want people to remember you even when you lose your existence.
And if you want to make it happen, do things which are marvellous; do things which are unforgettable. You need to make big contributions to the society so as to be remembered even when you're gone!
You need to do great deeds to be history. You need to make your hustle turn into success so that people bring up your name when they talk about the achievers from the past!
So, in order to be remembered and not to be forgotten, you are required to prove yourself! You are required to showcase your seity.

7. Because you are a human!
~You are a human and this makes you more susceptible of doing things. It turns out to be a bigger responsibility for you to do justice to your genera.~
As a human you are inexorably responsible for doing things that are given to the universe in bestowal.
You have been granted with innumerable abilities and so there's no wrong if you are expected to make contributions in the outer space.
Since you can sense the vibes and the signs that you are being given by the universe, you are supposed to make use of them. You are supposed to do the best possible things and return as much as you are able to understand!

8. Because your master is watching over you!
Now it's not just you who can create, there's a mightier

power that has created you!
And that power is always there, up! Watching down!
It is always looking after your life, it's always looking at you when you say you are stuck in a situation!
It tries to hint you, sneekily, squueshly, and ifff you are able to figure out those hidden gestures, you are able to solve most of the problems of this life.
And the point here is, that the one, that created you! Is expecting that you make use of all the tools and weapons that are given to you!
Love, faith, believe, potential, quality are the weapons that you are armed with and you are expected to make use of it to create something great out of this life.

9. Because if you can, why not!
   And there are no more questions to be asked as to why we should do it!
   You need to know your potential, know your field of interest and start working to make things happen in your way!

10. And! Because "That powerful play goes on and you can contribute a verse."

[13]
"Intution"

* * *

A form of thought that comes to us as vibes, vibes that give us a feeling of something that is about to happen!

Intuition are the sub-discipline of our thoughts, they render certain feelings within our auto suggest mechanism which often helps us to predict things.

Yes! One can predict things, if you master the art of controlling your thoughts the next thing that you are going to encounter is intuitions.

Not only a single person is blessed with the series of intuitions; we all are alluded by life. But only those who are working on "art of living" are able to uncover such facts of life.

At every instant, life instigates us about what's coming next but only a few of us are able to see what's coming because rest of us are having closed minds.

~Not every individual is able to divulge the secrets of life. Because not all of us believe in mysteries. We get constant gestures from the universe but only a few of us are in our senses to be able to realise them. ~

As I have shared most of my emotions with you; I now find it congenial to share some more weird verities of my life. I have always been a 'that was a sign' kinda person. As I evolved, I realised that everything that happens around me is leaving a sly innuendoes.

And every time I am able to notice any of these hints I am able to solve another riddle of this life for myself.

Out of many, one thing that I have discovered is that life of a single person is set on a set of numbers and alphabets.

The person I crushed upon as a kid came into my life on 18th, and since then for at least next two years I had started noticing the dates and every good thing would come to me one the even days. And over time I noticed that everything in my life made a move towards me on just even days including one odd number, 1.

My birth date 4 and other numbers,. 6 and 8 had been the most crucial numbers of my life. As I began to notice this thing I was then forced to relate all the happenings of my life to these no's.

My answer sheet number for exam would always end or begin with these numbers, so were the numbers of the hotels that I'd ever get in!

Also, the alphabets A and S have been the only alphabets that were related or a part of my attraction orbitals.

This is not a random thing, we all have a fixed 'algebra of life'.

Ever noticed? If you start counting on something time and again, it happens in the same way then? It is more than a mere coincidence. It is the 'algebra' of your life and if you'd find it for yourself then you yourself won't be attracted to the remaining values!

Once you figure out the values that are a part of your equation, it'd be all sorted! Your equations won't get puzzled up!

TINY BOIY!

As we move ahead I want you to mark down this homework for you!

What is the algebraic equation of your life?

You don't have know this for me or anyone but yourself!

-

This strong force of intuition which has been guiding me, I don't know ever since when. It has been my digger, it is helping me to dug out the treasures of life which are not really deep, they are on surface but they do need deep meditation! Deep concentration! To be acknowledged.

I've never had let go anything that came to me! I was always a keen learner.

I've always tried to think of the 'nonpossible' just like a word, I like to look for things which don't exist.

Whatever I say! It's nothing more than knowledge, motivation or entertainment to you but at the same time I find life in these words.

And I am not going to let go of you TINY! At least not till you say, "I'll find rarities in my life now, they may not be mindful for others but they are in my life, I am going to find them out."

The intuitions I'm talking about did not come as clear nightmares, they were not written on boards, they were not heard out loud on the bumping out loud JBL's. They were hidden! They were quiet, they were shy to come out because they didn't want people to seek them.

But they were beautiful li'l kid, worth being raised!

Raised to big bums! Dope-ass-bums. They had that spark, which lightened up the path ahead.

My sister never shared her secrets with me till I was some 14 years old.

At first I had to uncover her secrets on my own, but as I grew up, she began to share it all with me, all by herself.

I remember the times when she'd tell me of some guy and I'd promptly say some number of months, saying it like, 3! It's not going to last for more than three months and it strangely it ended up by three months.

We'd laugh at the silly presumption I'd make.

But it happened again! Not just one or two times! But always! Now this was something serious.

I had to chew over this happening to provide edification to myself. There was something that made me know about the person just by meeting him for once. I had always been able to know people for what they are at the insides, just after that one failure I never failed to know people!

~God made me get played once, just to ensure that I become the coach for the rest of my life! ~

And not just for my sister I was able to do this for everyone who was an element of my process in anyway. I would go wrong in anyway but not in telling if the two people had that harmonic connection between them or not! I've helped people with his power as much as I could.

And with this, I even tried to bring together, the real souls which were counteracts of each other.

And what I am trying to tell you is that I've always had a gospel in the signs of nature. So should you!

You know what? I might be wrong in all my illusions but the life I'm living is heaven. My beliefs are so strong that I'm never let down by the powers that I believe in. Anything could be wrong about my equations but that teacher over there is always making things go right in my way!

~Till the time you are sane, you are losing out a lot of things! Your consciousness won't let you trust in things that are unheard of. And to be able to encounter the things that are not talked about you need to get mad!~

~I closed my eyes, to not see them,
I played loud music, to not hear them.
My visions were of my own,
My songs had lyrics of my own.
I was floating',
They were boating'.
-
Drifting' water, sun shinier, even hotter,
Sky so close, almost in my hand,
Tell me what yae wants? I got the wand.
-
All the magic in tis air,
Everyone screaming' the game was fair.
Ladies in them fairy gowns,
As I look down I see clowns.~

[14] Your Love!

~Is yours!

Just yours, always yours, it might not be a body but always the soul.~

And when I have talked to you about everything how can I let the most alluring topic go unnoticed?

I know this is the area which needs to be given the maxim of limelight. Ain't this true?

~We all are living a life of romantics, we were born romantics, we can unlearn anything but not romance. No matter what! Opposite sex has always attracted us! It has always given us some fairy dreams.~

Your love shall be head over heels for your beloved. Your love shall be endless; your love shall be pure as the freshly driven snow.

You don't have to be in one hell of a hurry to find your love, you need to hush down! Finding your soul mate is not your job. It's the universe that's going to make it happen! Yes! You need to trust me on this too!

Having your soul mate to next to you is the most spiritual phenomenon of this universe. It's not our human efforts that are making it happen. It's the space that's making all the efforts to bring your counterpart to you.

It's may sound like another fantasy! But this is how the table the table for love is set! And this table can't be turned over.

~Cause our spirits were made in space and our counterparts have a log over their! I do sound off my rocker in all my talks, but i've got method to my madness.~

We all are constantly hustling to find the right soul mate for us. We are rushing because we lack that contentedness, we lack the feeling of faith in our powers.

Because it's taking too long for our true soulmate to come over, we are rushing into temporary relationships. And in spite of giving whole nine yards into those relationships we are coming out with nothing and then we feel the life is playing on us.

But the thing is that are beliefs are weak, we are impatient. We don't really trust ourselves enough to able to find the best for us. As a last resort; we pick our partners as they come in.

As a kid we imagine the dream guy for us.

One who'd come over to us out of the thin air onto his white horse. With a kind of face that'd stop you in your tracks, women would flock to him cause of his mystique, somewhat a big shot or an action hero at times. Somebody who's the playboy when in sacks and a buffoon; when it comes to responsibilities.

Somebody who gets to know what our heart feels without our mouth spilling it out.

Understanding, cute, hot, smart, loving, caring,

masculine, protective brap brap brap brapppp!!

And as we grow up, life happens!

And booomm!

We give up on our dream guy! We lose faith and just to make sure that we reach somewhere, we board any of the boat that comes over.

And when we reach the final destination, we end up somewhere where we don't want to be!

So tell me why? Why do you have to end up anywhere but your dream park?

Why is it easy for you to let go of your dreams?

Every day we are giving up on something that could have been ours but our lack of faith burned that bridge for us! And that is where we are losing the things that could have been ours for real!

Our weakness is our impatience; we are not ready to wait. Wait enough for the right things to come over.

My impatience is my favourite! It has helped me have things in my life, just when I want them. Because I've always made sure that my impatience doesn't get me split milk. And that is what you need to tell yourself. You have to know what things in your life need to be given a call off and what are the things that should be rushed onto.

As they say-'life can only be understood backwards', we are not able to figure out the situations while we are in them but only when we are over them.

~But a few things in life can be averted by our inner powers. We can have a control over most of the happenings of our life, we can decide whether we want to be a part of certain situations or not.~

For if you are thinking how to know that the person who you gonna get along with is meant for you or not. Then I want you to first laugh at yourself.

Mm hm.

Laugh TINY!!

Because it's you who should be telling which soul is going to dance on your melodies.

Meeting of two souls is surreal, you'd hear two planets almost colliding.

You'd feel the sky under your feet. It is going to be like a crazy dream. It's not going to happen outside, it'll be all within. And we cannot feel this magic if we did not meditate for this.

Instead of looking over any passerby you need to imagine a man of your own, a soul that'll be dragged to you by all the forces because it'll belong to you.

Dream of the teensy things of that dream soul, from the way it'd walk up to you to the way he'd walk all by him-self.

~Dream of the way he'd speak to you and won't speak to any of your friends. Dream, how he'd be the most stubborn soul with all the deep feelings hidden inside. Dream of how he'd be a mystery to rest of the world like you are. Dream how he'd be an ocean full of thoughts that'd compliment the tides within you. Dream of how he'd be aware of every single thought of yours. Dream, how he'd be revealing all his crimes to you and how you'd let him behind the closed doors of your heart. The person you'd want to be the reason of your pain, how you'd want him to rip out your soul and lose everything if need be.~

A man who'd always be telling the world about his love. Who'd tell you every day that your soul is the most be-numb-ing treasure that he has ever come across. How he'd make you bite your lips as his hands would move over your body. How he'd talk to you in language of body when you'd say "I don't want to talk".

~Dream of somebody who'd talk love not sex.~

Dream of the man you'd run up for, every day, every time, always and forever.

Your love would make you have a sip of heaven as his tongue would wrap around yours. Your love would make you taste serenity as his hands would move across your body, it will fix your soul from all the damages of your past, it'll make your heart beat louder at a moment and it'd simply make you skip a beat at the other.

It's going to be more than anything ordinary, 'cause ordinary isn't love!

And till the time you don't find a match to the extremities of your soul, you don't have to accept that love.

You don't have to get restless and pick any boat that comes over, you have to be patient enough to be by your side even if the boat doesn't arrives.

You don't have to tell yourself to wait for right love but to love yourself instead.

What you need to do in the first place is to marry yourself before you marry your love. Because no other person can bring that peace in your soul till the time you don't do that for yourself.

You need to marry yourself (just a thought that I stole from a TED talk.) and promise yourself that you'd be giving you all the love that is endeared by your spirit. Because you! Will never hurt yourself, your happiness will last when you'll be in self-love. You'd do more of things that your psyche needs.

Make yourself your first love. Love yourself enough to be happy! Love yourself so that you'll know what's remaining and what's left in your love that could come only from outside.

And once you know what your soul is looking for, you'd be screaming it out to the space, and the universe is going to work upon that piece, which is hidden somewhere and it'd be sent to you just when you'd be aware of its home-coming .

-

Your love is out for a walk! It'd be coming don't let anyone else in! May be he lost the track, but he'll be back.

Just when you will be about to settle for anything else, remind yourself; you the shit mama! You ain't settling for anything that does not counterparts your soul.

(May your beliefs remain strong, may you have your real soulmate.)

TINY!

No matter if you are girl or boy! The process of your love has to be same!

Be patient!

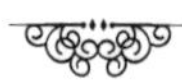

And....

* * *

It ticks me off to see people lacking faith in them!

I have said this many times rather all the times throughout this book that you need to `have faith in yourself'.

I personally find it crazy that people are so into the game of believing in others and not themselves.

I'm saying this cause I've been watching over them. It has been a few years since I have been trying to help my friends with their petty life issues.

I have been consoling and telling them of life as much as I have known. It may or may not be everything but it is something for sure.

But I still feel bad at times since I get to see that how they trust me so easily for the things I say and for the views I have! They got ain't no visions and it is not because they can't have it but because they are not willing to find out something new! They find it more feasible to cry over the situations instead of finding an optimistic way out!

~Your mind will always be able to give a positive stimulus even to the negative things if you have built it up with the bricks of optimism.~

As soon as you master the art of 'controlling your thoughts' you'll be able to live a controlled life. And you trust me on this you can shape up your entire life out of your thought bubbles into the reality.

It is upto us how we react to the situation, we can cry over that split milk for our entire life if we need just a reason to cry for and if we want to make something out of that then we can make that yummy home-made cheese.

What I'm trying to say is, that if crying is all you want to do, then you can cry over any damned thing! You can cry over the nail of yours that just got broke or for a reason as big as death of your beloved.

But!! What has happened has happened. That moment is gone! And why do we have to keep ourselves stuck in that moment?

It is a beautiful journey when you travel in this life with a controlled mind. When you decide that you are the master of your fate, when you decide that only I can decide the things that can affect me. When you are aware of the things you want and how you are going to nail it at the right stance.

I have been judged over everything, I have been told that I cannot make a way to big things!

But the only thing I could ever hear was what I told my brain, that I can be anything and everything that I want.

~ Ever since I decided they are just a matter to my plot and have no role in my story, they were not able to affect me at all!~

.

~Whatever I did was without worries! I just stopped worrying about people; the only thing I focussed on was myself! The focus was selfish not mean!~

You need to know the difference, everything I do is limited to myself. And when I am self-focussed I make sure that I'm not involving people in my way. My way to my goals is individual, people may accompany me at different roads but the journey is of my own. And as I go by these roads, I make memories with these passer-by's but I don't make them a way to my destination.

They are to complete me but then they are not a part of me!

~They will depreciate me, appreciate me, they will just give me some matter and it is up to me how I decide to use that in my story! Whether I let them be a mere crowd or the lead role of my story! ~

~But when I am the star, why shall I let them shine in my story?~

We all need to know this!

You!!!! Got to know this; TINY!

We all need to start a life for ourselves!

We need to stop going along with the society W\we need to be a rare matter because that's what we really are!

~Since the shine of other gems around is appealing us, we are polishing ourselves like others! We are losing our authenticity, we could have been something more than diamonds but we have decided to settle for diamonds.~

~We need to not settle! We need to keep going , going without knowing! Expect to be surprised by the life and it, for sure would leave you speechless!~

So if you are a grown up and have children and in any way you are contributing in the society then I want you to make a non-judgemental and an open to acceptance kind-of matter for the society! I want you to spread your share of positivity!

If you don't like something or if you don't agree

with something then you don't have to convince people to have a same perspective on that thing.

You don't have to throw a shade of your pessimism on people.

You don't have to try making other people concur with your thought! ~You have to stop spreading your thought! So that it doesn't becomes a vision to the buds that are being brought up by you!~

And if you are that blooming blossom who'll be producing a new life someday then I want you to varnish your thoughts. I want you to be the best vibes-giver. I want you to spread strong optimism and keep hold of your conceived notions to yourself.

If you give birth to a baby, don't tell them of stars being stars, just don't tell them nothing. Let them tell you what they have to say!

Let them give strange meanings to everything, let them have their own visions. Don't tell them people with breasts are female and the ones with a penis are male. Don't tell them males have to be strong and females have to look after homes.

Don't hide! tell them that fucking someone could not be a way to hurt them! It's just a way of loving ! Don't tell them raping a woman can affect her in any way! Don't tell them you have to talk low when you talk of a few things.

Make sure, that you are not telling, them that middle fingers are a slang! Because then they'll laugh at you when they'll find nothing abusive in the things that we are always hiding!

Don't tell them that you have to study first to be a successful person. Don't tell them that they need money to have everything.

Just don't tell them what is good and what's bad, just let them fall into those bad phases and realise that it's not good.

Don't yell at them when they talk of something wrong, don't stop them just let them be. Only if they will have strong minds; they will be a rebel.

Just feed their brains with strength! Strength of being truthful and the strength of never giving up.

Tell them it's all okay! Tell them that you want them to tell you.

Tell them not to get disheartened ever! Tell them not to cry over situations but laugh because you know you are going to knock it down.

Tell them that they are the only stars and they are unique. Tell them that whatever they'll think, they'll have it. Tell them to keep working hard and not giving up.

Tell them not to hurt others. Tell them to spread love and not cheat.

Tell them to not envy others because they have 'potential' which can beget them ever more.

Tell them they are treasures, they are powerful beyond measures and they can have everything that their mind can conceive.

Tell them to fear only one thing that is the power that created them and owns them. Tell them to discover if they find some power in their lives on their own.

Tell them to never give up on themselves because their life is a precious gift. As you raise your kid tell them that you don't expect anything from them.

Tell them you are happy to have them and you don't want them to change them for anything.

Tell them to embrace their flaws. Tell them that if it's not a good day today tomorrow the sun will shine again and when you wake up, you need to give up on last night's penitence. Tell them, 'What might have happened yesterday cannot ruin your tomorrow'.

And as you tell them I'll tell this to you again!

That you too are the BEST OF YOUR KIND!

You are perfect TINY!

You have enough of love! Your creators love you! Your friends love you!

If you don't feel their love! Here I'm sending my love to you!

I love you!

As I take a leave from you all I want to say is that it was a privilege for me to be able to encourage you even in the tiniest possible way. I know as a reader this privilege and thankful talks must be all shit to you, Ik! But when you are writing; you do find it a privilege that somebody just went through your long-winded series of vindication! And you feel thankful!

But, the only message that I had for you was that, you don't have to hold yourself from designing your own crazy concept for this life! And you don't need no person to believe in you, because what you need is yourself!

A strong mind is always able to attract others, and if your beliefs are strong and undeviated, society itself will be attracted to you!

Your aim should be to find a meaning of you and your life on your own.

Whatever I said was my meaning to life! And you can decide yours.

I hope to get along with you soon!

And I know you'd also be waiting to meet me by the time I make my next visit here!

I wish that you make it possible for yourself to live an unfiltered life and this time on your own terms!

XOXO,

Sonali & Li.

REMINDER.

'KNOW YOURSELF. BELIEVE IN YOURSELF AND YOUR POWERS.'

"COME OUT OF THEIR TRAP!"

Goodbye till i see you next!!
Stay happy, and be your best!!

"I smile to the karma and she smiles back at me!!"

* * *

5:30 and the bus haven't started yet!

What are they doing? My head was having talks as I gazed upon a group of 5 foreigners sitting on the footpath, waiting for the bus to get started.

The group had three girls and two were the boys. All the girls had their back towards me while the guys had their faces in my direction.

One of those girls donned an amazing water tattoo at the back of her arm and another Egyptian tattoo at the back of her neck which intrigued me to keep looking at them.

I was killing my time, so were they!

The girl at the extreme left took out her pretty white and long cigarette that for sure did not belong to India. She offered it to the remaining people in the group and they smoked away the time.

Raju travellers!
Cmon, everybody!
Come inside!
Yelled the bus conductor.

`Yes ma'am? Your ticket?' he enquired to me.

I showed my pay tm message in return.

Okay keep your luggage in the in the luggage storage, replied the conductor.

I went back, out of the bus to give my luggage!

Backpack on my back, an over-flooded handbag and a sling on each side with a water bottle in my hand. And it just fell off! Just all of it!

I picked up the sling, and placed my backpack in the storage and the water bottle was lying in the feet of the girl that I just saw smoking cigarette, I looked up to her thinking may be she'd lift that up for me.

She was hesitant and tried to avoid any indulgence in the moment!

I lifted my bottle, placed the remaining luggage; went back to the bus!

28!

Seat no. 28, come ma'am, this way!

That statuesque girl followed me!

"Make these girls sit together" said a voice, from the team of the bus managers.

'Ma'am, this is yours and ma'am you sit there', superintended the conductor.

'I want window seat!,' I said.

Sorry, ma'am you have seat no.28, it doesn't have a window.

Okay! I replied in all the disappointment.

You get in first, I alluded the girl with a smile. She for sure had the most riparian smile; I noticed as she smiled back at me.

And we both got seated. I adjusted my handbag under the seats, placed my bottle in that elastic bottle holder place looking at the girl just the way she did and got settled in my place.

Are you comfortable? I asked the girl. As to know if my bags and other placements were not causing her any trouble.

Yahhh! Perfectly! She replied with a smile that showcased a tinge of her dimple this time.

Okay! I smiled back.

Where are you from? I asked the girl!

As the curiosity had hit me already!

Israel! She replied.

Oh! Okay! So for how long have you been here in Delhi?

2 months! The girl replied.

Well that's nice, so are you also heading to manali? I enquired.

No, Kasol! I'm going to Kasol she said.

Oh that's cool. So you came here alone? Like to India?

Yah! I just finished my elmi# and came to India!

Sorry? I begged pardon.

I completed my almi#! And came here after it just got completed.

Sorry? I mean what did you complete? Army! Did you say Army?

Yes Army! She replied.

Oh okay! That's amazing, but how did you complete army?

I mean are you done with that? Was that a course! What did you do in army?

Yes! I completed my army. Most of the girls in Israel do army and the boys do @@$^*.

I could not get what guys there did!

What's your age? She asked me?

20, I replied! ......And what's yours?

21! She said.

Not a big difference I said, as I asked another question. So how many places have you been to in India?

That patriotic me had to a lot to ask that day!

None, said the girl.

None? Who have been nowhere since two months?

Noo! It's my firrrst day here!

But you said you've been here since past two months? I questioned back!

No! I'm here for next two months that's what I meant!

Oh! Okay!!!!!! So you mean that this is your first day in India?

Yes!

Woah! So how have you been? How was your journey till here?

She started..

It was nice! I got to my hotel as I touched down here!

Got fresh n up to catch my bus for kasol! I went to have a pizza before coming here! I met a young boy there he helped me to find the way to my ola cab!

People are nice here! She ended.

Oh! Yea!! Hm!!! Was how I kept responding.

And a silence came to mark its attendance after a long conversation!

.

.

So what's your name? Asked the girl to me!

Sonali! I replied.

Ohh! Like Sonali like Manali?

Hahha yea!

And what's yours? I asked.

Re3#$@!

SORRY? I couldn't get that!

@#at@!

Mmmm.. How do you write it?

RENATA!

Oh okay! But I'm going to forget it! I said as I gave a witty smile.

Hahha, she joined.

But I won't forget yours, Sonali, Manali! She replied and we both busted out laughing even harder together!

And silence made its way back.

Okay i've got to sleep! I'm going to see you in a while! I said!

Goodnight she replied!

You are also going to sleep? I questioned her.

Mmm yes! May be.

Okay! Goodnight then!

I tried to shut my eyes and get some sleep!

It was in no way that I could get a hold of that utterly desired sleep! I kept changing positions of my head from one side to the other. But sleep had no mercy on me! She wasn't ready to come!

My eyes pained but thoughts were spinning!

One hour gone! I was still struggling to call that sleep. As I looked at my partner, she was asleep!

And I kept struggling for another one more hour to get some sleep!

But our relationship had been on real hardships! Because I always romanced with my mind so much that it used to get jealous and would never come to meet me when I'd ask!

2 hours down! She got up!

You didn't sleep?

Mmhm! Tried to!

Oh! I was asleep!

Ya I saw that!

I want to pee! I added.

But you can't? Where would they stop the bus?

I don't know where the next stop would be;

Mmmmm.. M controlling!!!; I almost moaned.

Ahh!! You know? If it'd have been in Israel the person would have started screaming out here!! Like "stop the bus, I need to pee!!" she mimicked some weirdsome voice.

'We cooperate and adjust in India' I said!

"Yeahh! I just saw that! That's really nice!" She concurred to my words.

So can we stop talking about how my urinay bladder is about to undergo an explosion and just change the topic?? I requested.

Hahha yes!

Yah! so tell me something about yourself! I asked with utmost curiosity, to know more of her.

What about myself?

Like anything; what do you love the most?

I love sea! I love visiting seas!

Damn!! I would love to do that as well but sadly, there are no seas in Delhi. I have never been to a sea! I replied with all promptness.

Really? You have never been to a sea? She questioned surprisingly.

Mmhnm! We don't have such scenic beauty in Delhi and I have rarely been out of Delhi!

Hmmm

So what do you hate? I questioned again.

I hate bad people!

Oh! But anyone would hate bad people!

"Who do you think are bad people? Like what makes you call a person bad? " I went on with my series of questions.

``Umm, the ones who act like they are your friends but they are not really your friends! The one who talk bad about you when you are not there!" she hinted.

Oh! You mean back-bitchers?

Yes! she said.

Alrighttttttt!

What's that thing on your hand, I asked her as I saw the mehndi on her hands, It had a beautifully crafted 'Om' symbol on the backside of her hand.

Yess!! I got it! She remarked.

From where did you get this done?

Main bazaar she said!

Alright, that seems cool!

What do you call thankyou in hindi? She enquired.

Shukriya! I said!

No that's said by muslims! She negated.

And I promptly corrected myself, 'dhanyawad' ! Dhanyawad is the word!

Yea! That one! Daaanyawad!

Daanyawad! I will remember this now!

.

..

You hungry? .

No! I'm not.

I took out my box of biscuits and punjabi tadka!

Have some, I said.

Oh, she said as she picked a biscuit.

So what do you call it?

Oh! These are chips and she pointed the biscuits calling them butter cookies!

I said `so that's nothing new.'

And we laughed together.

Wait! I too have something to eat, lemme get that out for you!

"No, no! I don't want to have anything rn!" I said!

"No! It's most wanted Isralian snack! Taste it!" she pleaded.

She took out a small packed of the puffed corns.

We call it bamba! She said as she extended that packet to me!

What?

B-amb-a she repeated!

Bamba! Okay!! I said!!

How's it?

Cool! (It had that Indian kurkure puffcorn taste just that it wasn't spicy unlike Indian stuff!)

It was nice I said!

.

A 10 second pause and I popped up another question!

So what about your family?

.

I have one elder sister and one brother and I'm the youngest one!

Oh! Even I have one elder sister and one younger brother, I'm the middle one!

That's great. What about your parents? I asked her!

My mother passed away when I was 10 and our father doesn't live with us anymore

.

Oh! I said. What did you do after that? I asked instead of showing any condolence because that was actually what I wanted to know?

I raised myself up! She said

And that is what I wanted to hear!

What did you do after that one bad stance? I asked to hear more from her.

I started working when I was 14.

"So u paid for your education all by yourself?" I bumped in another question.

Not really! Goverment provides some fund for such children in Israel. And I got some help from that as well!

I completed my Army, I want to serve my nation. I want to help poor kids and provide aid to those who are in need!

Words continued to fall out of her mouth,

But I could hear nothing! I could only see a strong woman, who decided to get armed by the pains of her life instead of being wounded.

A girl who decided not to become a victim of the downfall that life gave her.

She had the prettiest smile with a smeary shade of dimples, which talked of all the beauty in life and no pain!

It's a stop!!

A sudden announcement was made by one man from the team of bus managers in Hindi.

"Oh let's get off!" I replied in bewilderment.

Why? She said!

It's a stop I told her.

Okay let me take my cigarettes she said!

Ya sure, I waited.

And we both stepped out of the bus together.

'Let's go to the washroom first', I said.

Yessss! She replied.

We came back.

And went into the dhabba, I helped her out with the menu!

I tried to explain her the dishes and we successfully made it! And had our complete dinner.

We moved out and clicked a lot of pictures!

And as we got done with all of that I said, 'let's go there! You can smoke there'

I pointed towards a place where two of our bus mates were already smoking.

As she puffed away her cigarette, she questioned; "so you don't smoke?"

"No," I said.

"You smoke no weed, no marijuana no nothing?"

No I said! Laughing hard as I looked how freaked out she was to hear this!

But why?

I have never been fascinated by these things I said.

Mmm... Nice!!! She replied with more of surprise.

Her cigarette was almost done when the conductor yelled, 'time is over'.

I told her we need to get back, break time is up!

O yea! Let's rush then she said!

We headed back to our seats!

I want the window seat this time!! I declared!

Hahah sure! She laughed back!

I got my window seat!

"Send pictures! Now!" I said impatiently.

We exchanged the photographs, phone numbers and more of laughters.

.

.

I told her that I'm writing a novel!

"That's nice what is it about?" she delved.

It's about the countless meanings that life has!

It's for those who have limited their visions to a certain ideas and are not really open to other verses!

I went on with a 5 minute speech I believe!

I agree with you! She said in ratification when it ended!

And she suddenly picked up her backpack that was lying under our seats.

As she looked for something in her bag and could not find because of dim lights, I offered her my water bottle thinking that she was looking for water!

No, she said. And took out a small diary and a pen at the next moment!!!

And I was like!! Oh!! So you write too?

No, not like you but I do write to myself at times!

She started turning pages!

"Would you read that out to me?

If you don't mind?" I asked with intrusiveness.

I had all the audacity of knowing about the hardships and peaks that she has had in her life!

Okay let me find something she went through the pages and asked me to flash the light from my phone on the diary as to make it visible.

I could see something and get nothing.

What language is that!

321$%@ she said.

'Alright' I replied!

Uh, this! Okay! She opened a page of when she was some 12 year old.

And she read another which was dated on 6th of the January of the year that was continuing.

She'd read it in her language and translate it back to me in English!

There were some lines that she mumbled and could not exactly turn them into English, but we successfully retrieved all the emotions that lied there in those pages!!

.

.

Awww!! I'm proud of you!!

You are a real nice soul, I said as she finished reading!

She gave that broad and mighty smile.

You tell me now? Something about yourself. She bombed mee now!

Mm.. What?

So what about your family?

Family? I have a perfect and happy family. We are five people my mom, my dad my sister and brother!

In India, we are like more of family oriented people! I said.

We do everything according to our families and if not then it's according to the society!

Okay! So why aren't you going with your friend to Manali? She further questioned.

I don't really have friends and I enjoy more of my own time!

Also, my parents don't know that I'm going to such a far-off place alone!

Then what did you tell them as to when you left from home? She inquired.

'I told them that I'm leaving for hostel", I replied.

Ohhh! Smart! She said.

And we laughed!

India is too big! She said as to break our monotony.

Mhmhm. I said. How big is Israel? I questioned back!

Israel is very small! You can fly across entire Israel

in 3-7 hours!

That's small!! I said!

Yea, she nodded.

Soo.... What did you like about India

People here are very sweet..

And?

Mountains! There's lot of scenic beauty here!

And what did you hate?

The drivers, they panic a lot!!

What else?

I don't know it's my first day as of now, she remarked.

O yah! And then you'll be having an endless list of like and dislikes by the end of your two months!

And we exchanged laughs together as she agreed.

And silence stroked!

I started looking out of the window! We were into the mountains now!!

It was all dark outside! There were rarely any lights!

Gigantic rocks, non-symmetric roads, walls with no tessellation, freezing breeze and heart-throbbing vibes!

They all caught me altogether!

~There were heights around me and I was sinking inside me, into the deepest thoughts of all the times!~

I thought of life, nature, strength, positivity, god and! The girl sitting next to me!

I should write about her! Said my thought!

I turned up to her and said, "Will you please translate your diary again? So that i can write it down for myself?"

Where it come from? She asked with a big question mark!

`Sudden thought!' I said as I shrugged my shoulders.

Um.. Sure!!!

The diary was lying next to us!

I picked it up for her, and she made a hold of it!!

Same struggle yet again!

Flashlight turned on, paper pens out!! Recollecting connecting words from that Arabic language to English!

And here is, what we recollected!

(Diary on two different days, from the same girl! Situations were same, but she decided to have an optimistic approach to the same situations after a period of almost ten years. She decided not to complain and to love herself instead.)

June, 2006

My diary,

I want to tell you that you are my best friend and even more my sister and everybody else.

I can't tell how safe I feel with you and I want to tell you all the stuff that I save in my heart.

My brother has started working in pizza and he is home just in night.

My sister also comes to home just in night and we do nothing!

I am angry because I think my sister loves his boyfriend more than me! I hate it that in the night she speaks with her boyfriend.

They (my sister and her boyfriend) get enough time together but what about us? ? ?

We spend no time together!

It's very hard to be alone! !

Bye!

06 January, 2017

Hey Yoni!

Remember me? ?

Renata!

The same girl but I have changed.

May be you didn't even recognise me!

It's funny to read the past! The same past that has made me what I am today.

It was a lot of pain and suffering!

But today, it's all beautiful.

I finished the Army and now it's just me to myself.

This life is a shit and I know it but I found myself. And I am not looking to be like everyone else.

Today, I do only those things that make me feel good!

I try to be around good people, with a good energy

" I smile to the karma and she smiles back to me!!"

A lot of things about this life are bad, but it's good to me, I feel good.

The next time I'll open you, I'll be in a better place!

-huge love!

And she was in the best place, 'in India , sitting right next to me!' I said sarcastically and we both busted in laughter all over again!

We switched off the lights and I went back to my thoughts and she went off to her sleep.

I thought of giving her a gift! A remembrance of mine because she had given me a good happy life short story!

I thought of the one white netted top that I had brought along! And decided to give that to her before she'd go down on her stop!!

And it was about to come to an end!

Our journey together!

`Packup! People heading to Kasol!' an announcement was made.

We both got up and I helped her in getting her stuff

together, I gave her that one top now! And took out my notepad to give her a letter!

Hey Renata!

You are one of the pure souls that my life has brought to me.

You have the prettiest smile and I want you to keep flaunting that smile forever!!

Also, never stop telling yourself in the mirror that you love yourself and you are perfect, like you already do!

May your life get you the best of a future!

Welcome to India!!

Have fun in Kasol.

Sonali Sharma.

"I'm not going to read this right now." She said as I handed it over to her.

Reading her stuff when she was in different verses of her life, that's what she liked!

Wait, I have to give you something in return!

No you don't have to I negated.

Ah, right here, she took of the purple gemstone necklace that she was wearing and made me wear it!

It's for you!

Awh! Thankyou so much I said and we hugged!

.

And it was the time!

Bus stopped, and she was leaving, leaving a small stance to me, few more thoughts in my mind and one more verse to my story!

She got up and gave me a warm hug!!

It was real! I could feel all the warm vibes, I could feel the sense of purity and sanity in that hug!! It wasn't ordinary, it was a real thanksgiving between two souls.

-

And we walked our steps!

Finally out of the bus!

Pure blue skies, cold breeze, beautifully painted rocks, craftily pasted together one over the other, raised miles above the land!

Nature was doing magic there! The air was romantic enough to leave anyone breathless!

The senses of the place were soothing enough to rip out your soul, to put on some glitters, flowers and showers on it and put it back into your body!!

A place where your heart would almost leave your skin and would tell you that I'm going to stay here and won't go along when you'll go back to your homeland!

Everything so serene! Full of life!

It was all heavenly!

~It was a feeling, it was not words!~

It was that talk that couples make when they don't talk! It was the talk between the soul and the heaven!

It was dreamy, dreamy enough that you'd force yourself back to sleep not to come out of that dream.

It was a moment of serendipity, it was all uncalled for! It was the best of what a person could really want from life!!

Because the nature ruled here! It was a nomans land! It did not allow any evil!

It was close to the skies and angels were dancing there.

5. am in the morning!

Mountains on both the sides and we were somewhere in between.

Not just in between of the roads between cities not in between countries, lands or skies but in between life!

We were living in a beautiful phase of our life!!

.

And we were out to bid the final good-bye!

Hugs exchanged again! Vibes flowed, chest to chest. Melancholy repeated in between the two souls.

Love rendered, body to body. Stories shared, mind to mind.

.

And she was gone!

.

And I was two hours away from my destination!

And I tried to put the whole journey into words in those two hours, so that I could tell you about a girl!

A girl, who was betrayed by life at an age of as young as 10 years old!

She was left with no parents! Having no parents was not the reason of the pain!

Pain was because solitude spoke louder than companionship!

Pain was because the soul was not getting any love and body was given no care!

The pain was because the mind was becoming a victim of misfortunes!

The pain was not going away because, the seed of brokenness was sown very deep down inside.

It needed to be kindred by safety! It needed strength and stability.

The harshness of society was about to rip it off the roots. The society was not really kind to that one seed!

But the truth is; it was not the outer world that was not letting it grow!

It was its own insecurities that were not allowing it to come out and have a face-off with the harsh reality!

.

But it was not for a long time that this girl decided to cry alone in the darkness of the nights.

~She got up to add on her shine to the mornings outside!~

Just when she started telling herself that there was nothing that world could do for her and it was everything that she could do for herself, she was able to grow! Grow on the land that was barren externally!

~Her branches were now blooming! She flowered positivity, strength and self-belief!~

She didn't curse life anymore for the things she couldn't have instead of doing that she decided to celebrate everything' that she was given!

She told herself, every day that she had all she needed and she'd give herself whatever will be required!

She opted her own way to crumble the cookie, so that she'd blame nobody else for a bad result!

She no more waited for the ball to get into her court, she instead walked her way to the ball!

.

Life and the situations were the same, she did not get her parents back, she had no successful relationship!

But! What she had now was a better mind-set! She had better filters to see through!

She had self-love and so she did not long for others to love her!

She decided to smile at everything that'd come in her way! No matter how rude that thing is, she learned to smile at it!

She created an environment for her soul that had all the serenity and love!

That paradise was beautifully cultivated, with all the positive vibes and enormous love and she was the queen of her paradise!

She ruled like the queen 'R' and she lived like one!

Let's just be..

* * *

Let us all get together try to bring a revolutionary change!

Let's just forget everything we've ever known!

Let's start it all over again with a feeling of love!

Let us be regisseur of love! Let us create love and spread it across with no limits!

Let's just be a fragrance of happiness and let's just linger in each other's lives for no reason!

Let us just try to be our own amorists so that we can give away more of love when others seek it from us.

~Let us know about pain, let us try to be in its affinity for longer so that we cherish joy with more of gaiety!~

Let's spread no hate and share glee.

Let us for a moment, forget that we have any earthly relation and let's just try to lift ourselves from the space that we've always been in!

~Let us not believe that days are with the sun and nights are with the moon!

Let us not decide if stars belong to the moon or to

the sun!~

Let's get ready to give up on the dreams that we saw according to what we were told about this universe!

And let's just have new dreams full of enigma.

Let's just emphasise on the dreary jiffs instead of ignoring them!

~Let's try to face things that we've usually disregarded.~

Let's try to talk more of bad things! Let's talk of them so much that we no longer find anything bad in them!

Let us see good in every bad and let us make bad the new good!

Let's make it even easier, let's forget there is anything like bad and let's just keep looking for good and disregard everything that is not appealing!

-

-

Let us not be scared of being defeated, alone, sad!

Let us be afraid when we get no reason to be hurt and our heart gets to feel no pain!

~Let us not censor the sex scenes from the movies! Let us rather censor the intoxicating war scenes, let us censor the malefic thoughts that are given away from the hate shows.

Let us be afraid of teaching our kids about hatred, cruelty and lies instead of love, truth, kindness or even erotic teachings.~

Let us not decide anymore what a man should be about and who a woman should be.

~Let us worship our god from our souls and not bodies.~

~Let us have our own religion which has got no shade of the society and the things which aren't denuded by us.~

Let us not be that judgemental head that keeps on ticking people and the society for the way things are happening!

Let us create our own lives and be placid.

~Let's just be in a revolution!

A revolution that embellishes the camouflaged goodness in bad!~

Let's be a part of this badass revolution together!

TINY!

I count you into the revolution of badassery!